Entrepreneur® **M**ADE **E**ASY *Series*

MEETINGS **M**ADE **E**ASY

The Ultimate Fix-It Guide

FRANCES MICALE

Ep
Entrepreneur®
Press

Editorial Director: Jere Calmes
Cover Design: Beth Hansen-Winter
Composition: CWL Publishing Enterprises, Inc., Madison, WI, www.cwlpub.com

This publication is designed to provide accurate and authoritative information in
regard to the subject matter covered. It is sold with the understanding that the
publisher is not engaged in rendering legal, accounting, or other professional services. If legal advice or other expert assistance is required, the services of a competent professional person should be sought.

—From a Declaration of Principles jointly adopted by
a Committee of the American Bar Association and
a Committee of Publishers and Associations

ISBN 1-932531-24-6

Library of Congress Cataloging-in-Publication Data
Micale, Frances A., 1954-
    Meetings made easy : the ultimate fix-it guide / Frances A. Micale.
        p. cm.
    Includes bibliographical references and index.
    ISBN 1-932531-24-6
    1. Meetings. I. Title.
HF5734.5.M527 2004
658.4'56--dc22

                                                                    2004057426

Printed in Canada

09 08 07 06 05   10 9 8 7 6 5 4 3 2 1

Contents

To Family

Especially Jim and Mary Beth

Foreword

Anything done well looks easy.

We've all heard this quote many times. And we've seen it in action when we watch star athletes, actors, or musicians perform magnificently with seemingly "effortless perfection." When I see such excellence, I am sometimes overcome with admiration, even adulation. I feel privileged to witness such outstanding performances.

Those are the same feelings I experience when I watch Francie Micale conduct a meeting. When she facilitates a session, the group quickly develops its own culture of professionalism, valued purpose, and focus of ideas, as well as a respectful exchange of facts, feelings, and views. The most fascinating aspect of the event is that each of them knows he or she is under the gentle but firm guidance of a consummate expert. It allows them to rise to even higher levels of performance.

As I read this book, I was reminded of a consulting engagement Francie and I conducted jointly a few years ago. I can hear Francie speaking to the group—all older men from the construction industry. Within minutes she had established a rock-solid credibility with this group of "good old boys." Yes, the fact that she is both attractive and charming helped, but those assets were overshadowed by her superb skills in facilitating.

The objective of this book is to share with you those concepts, skills, and techniques that work so beautifully for her. As an international management consultant, I have seen very few facilitators in her class; she practices what she preaches.

All you have to do now is study—yes, I said *study*—this book and apply what you learn here when you facilitate your next meeting. I guarantee that if you apply these techniques, you can expect to conduct a better meeting—and you will have fun doing it. Your group will undoubtedly say, "That meeting was conducted so well! We were on track and focused. And the facilitator made it look easy."

Peter A. Land
President
Peter A. Land Associates, Inc.

Introduction

During the late '70s, I worked for a supermarket chain called Food Giant, based in Atlanta. At one time, we had over 80 grocery stores in the Southeast. I was in charge of training, so I worked in the corporate office.

One Friday morning, my boss called me into his office and told me he had some bad news. I could tell something was wrong because his usually jovial and confident countenance had turned pale and somber. Then he said the company could no longer afford to do training and that I and my entire staff were being terminated.

This was pretty shocking—but it shouldn't have been. We had begun to lose market share, which resulted in closing some of our stores or selling them to independents. I had also heard store managers muttering about the latest operating policies and how they did not think they were going to bring in customers. This went on for a couple of years.

I encouraged everyone who expressed doubts to talk to their managers about it. After all, the people who worked closest to customers needed to be heard! But I was just as guilty as anyone else in refraining from expressing my concerns. I would go to weekly operational meetings in which the district managers and vice president of operations were all present. I rarely spoke my mind; I just sat there and listened.

If either I or store managers had spoken up during operational meetings, maybe things would have been different. At least there would have been other policy options to consider. But when an organization is run by top management without any consideration to employee opinion, there is no opportunity to think about other ways of doing things.

That's one reason why I wrote this book! I want to encourage business professionals to use meetings to create a forum for exploring all the options for an organization to follow. Only then can the best decisions be made.

Make It Important

When people do not perceive a meeting as important, they lose interest. And they'll do anything to get out of attending it—including asking an associate to page them during the meeting, to give them an excuse for leaving early in order to address "something important that has come up."

In order to conduct meetings that provide an interactive forum, it's critical to know how. Unfortunately, complaints about the quality of meetings are very common.

I conducted a survey in which I polled people at several levels within organizations, from vice president and above down to administrative positions. The results indicated that business professionals in general were dissatisfied with the quality of their meetings.

When asked how often their meetings achieved results, the average

> Meetings have become corporate America's favorite pastime!

response was 3.5, which is halfway between "sometimes" and "often." Since respondents indicated that the time spent in meetings is around 25 percent of the workweek, ineffective meetings can have a major impact on the success of an organization.

Why do companies hold so many meetings? In today's market, organizations must renew and even reinvent themselves to get or maintain a competitive edge. Change and upheaval are normal operating procedure. This necessitates keeping employees aware of current events so they can work toward the company's latest objectives. Also, murky waters muddle decision routes. So managers must gather ideas and opinions in order to choose effectively.

Gaining employee input whenever possible also increases the level of ownership. Most business professionals understand this, since survey respondents indicate that their meetings solicit input most of the time. They realize that this

Team Decisions

Heribert Stumpf, Business Unit Controller for Siemens in Atlanta, Georgia, says this about today's environment:

Business today is more complex than ever. One person cannot always know what the best decision is. In many issues, getting the input of others through a team decision process is most effective in today's environment.

practice motivates employees to make a stronger commitment by working harder and putting forth their best effort. It removes the barriers that limit people to doing only what is expected and unleashes their full potential so they help the organization prosper. The business meeting is seen as an ideal arena for making this happen.

Since meetings can be so important to an organization, effectiveness and productivity become critical issues. Survey respondents indicated three top reasons why meetings do not produce results:

1. The group doesn't follow the agenda.
2. There is no clear meeting objective.
3. There is no participation.

Much of the responsibility for the above problems and other challenges falls upon the person leading the session. It is therefore important for anyone who leads meetings to recognize and understand the possible roles and functions of meetings.

Generally, meetings serve two major functions: *sharing information* or *making decisions*. Each function requires the person who is in charge of conducting the meeting to play a different role.

Sharing information requires the person conducting the meeting to take on a *directive role*, since the group is simply receiving information. This is the traditional meeting that American companies have held for years and years. The person leading the meeting is there to present an idea or decision to the people attending the meeting. He or she directs the participants to action. These are some of the types of information that might be presented:

- ▶ The restructuring of an organization
- ▶ An assignment of new jobs or responsibilities
- ▶ An announcement of a decision made by management
- ▶ A new policy

Generally, meetings serve two major functions: sharing information or making decisions.

Staff meetings typically share information about current departmental events and performance. This type of meeting, while necessary at times, does not promote much commitment. People go to the meeting and carry out directives, yes, but they mostly just do what they are paid to do.

What About Staff Meetings?

Staff meetings generate a lot of negative reactions. People complain that they occur too often, never begin or end on time, are dominated by the boss, and are generally a waste of time.

Consider holding staff meetings less frequently and keeping them on a tight schedule. This will force you to focus on the most important issues. Get a different person to conduct the meeting each time. Solicit ideas from the group on what should be discussed at each meeting.

Meetings that focus on *making decisions* have the potential to be much more powerful. Participants become active and essential to running the organization. They are not just presented information; they are asked to make a decision together about something that affects the organization. This is done through the guidance of a *facilitator*.

Both *directive* and *facilitative* roles are important, but when to assume either or both roles depends upon the meeting objective. When people attend a meeting to make a decision, they are much more engaged in the meeting than when they are there to receive information. They have received the authority to participate, offer ideas, make decisions, and plan to implement them. But they need help in organizing their ideas and structuring their efforts. A facilitator can help them do so.

The *facilitator* is the person designated to help the group make decisions, solve problems, and develop and implement plans within the structure of a meeting. The facilitator should strive to create a comfortable atmosphere that encourages all members of the group to actively participate in discussions. The facilitator can also help coordinate the efforts of the members after the meeting.

Several years ago I learned the true significance of facilitation. I was hired to work with a medium-sized company in the Atlanta area. I was asked to help the company become more customer-focused and make some operational improvements.

Extending Beyond the Meeting

The facilitator's job continues even after the meeting ends. This is especially true when the facilitator is working with a group on a long-term project. These are some of his or her responsibilities outside the meetings:

▶ Getting more resources for the group
▶ Keeping senior managers and others informed
▶ Tracking results
▶ Establishing a strong business case for the group's work
▶ Coordinating activities as directed by the group

When I started working with the management team, I noticed the managers were not very excited about the prospect of working harder to make improvements. Actually, they were downright indifferent. I got the impression they did not like coming to work.

I knew I had a big job to accomplish, given the obstacles. I set to work scheduling and organizing problem-solving meetings. The idea was to help the managers develop their own plan for reaching specified goals. During the meetings I tried to create an environment in which everyone had an opportunity to speak honestly and openly and we would address all ideas in some way.

At first there was a lot of silence, but when people started realizing they could speak their minds with no fear of reprisal, they became fully engaged in the discussion. Little by little, the managers were able to work out their issues and problems. This extended into the front-line employees as well. Company communication improved, morale went up, and people became more proficient at solving problems.

There was one particular manager who changed dramatically. At first, he was the most skeptical and the most resistant toward the improvement effort. Yet, after attending the meetings, working closely with his peers, and seeing some of his own ideas being implemented, he realized that he could actually make a difference. He ended up being the biggest supporter of the improvement effort and was able to convince many other people to support it. They realized that they could really make a contribution and this resulted in significant advances within the company.

Effective facilitation is a key factor in helping people realize that they *do* have a say and *can* make difference. Members of the company I worked with described it quite well when they said that, as a facilitator, I guided them through the change effort. The credit for actually making the improvements went to the management team and everyone involved in the improvement effort. They carried out the actions. I just pointed the way through the process.

The Facilitator as Catalyst

A great facilitator doesn't have all the answers. The most important responsibility is to be a catalyst, guiding others toward accomplishments.

The facilitator's role can be complex. Being an effective facilitator takes some practice and even more effort. There is always something new to learn. This book focuses on how to facilitate groups to help the members work cohesively as they make decisions and bring them to fruition.

Decisions can be made around two types of situations: *business problems* and *business opportunities*.

A business *problem* is a situation in which something is not working properly. Examples are excessive errors in billing customers, key entry errors, incorrect service orders, equipment breakdowns, excessive delays, poor customer service ratings, low employee morale, and negative sales outcomes.

A business *opportunity* is a situation in which the group is to improve some aspect of the organization for growth and development. There is no problem, but there is an opportunity that calls for a decision that will make the organization better or more competitive. For example, company managers may decide, based upon changes in the market or customer demands, that it's time to introduce a new product or service. Other examples would be to increase market share, plan an event, or develop a new ad campaign.

Business *problems* usually require a group to do research on what is causing the problem. This activity is called *root cause analysis* and is necessary as a first step toward solving the problem. Business *opportunities* do not require root cause analysis, because they do not deal with situations in which something has gone wrong.

Here's an example of this difference. Suppose that you had a dead tree in your yard. That would be a problem. Before going out to buy a replacement tree, you would do a root cause analysis to find out why the tree died. If it was diseased, a new tree planted close by could also die. So you would not only be failing to solve the problem but also creating another problem. Now suppose you decided to buy a new tree for your yard. Nothing has happened to any of your existing trees; you just want to beautify your yard by adding more foliage around your house. That would be an example of an opportunity.

In order to facilitate a group competently toward solving *business problems* or addressing *business opportunities*, there are two things you must be able to manage—the meeting and the people.

Managing the Meeting

Whether you are directing or facilitating, you can manage a meeting most effectively by doing three things.

First, you must ensure that a meeting is even needed. Complaints about the number of unnecessary meetings are common. They waste valuable time and disrupt focus. This book will give you guidelines to prevent you from scheduling unnecessary meetings.

Scheduling Smarts

Nick Tate, editor for Science and Medicine at the *Atlanta Journal-Constitution* says, "Often someone will say we need to schedule a meeting to discuss a specific issue. I always make a point of asking if it would be possible to discuss the issue right now, while we're together. Many times, I am able to avoid having to schedule a meeting. That saves both parties a lot of time."

The second action is to prepare adequately for the meeting. It is great to have the visibility you get from being in charge of a meeting. However, the visibility when you're not prepared can divert attention from the issues being discussed and focus on you, unfavorably. In the pages ahead, you will learn specific steps necessary for preparing thoroughly without spending inordinate amounts of time.

The third necessary action is to conduct the meeting. The ensuing chapters will focus on specific steps for both beginning and ending a meeting. You will also learn ways to structure a group's approach toward reaching a specified goal.

Managing the Group

There are four competencies that will help you manage the group, which is most critical when your role is that of facilitator.

The first competency is remaining *content-neutral*. This means being completely unbiased about the ideas and opinions the group is expressing. This is sometimes difficult to do and it requires self-discipline. The groups I facilitate as a consultant are quick to let me know when I'm not being neutral. They don't need my opinions, only guidance in leading them through the agenda. It sometimes takes considerable effort to remain silent, but the group's positive response is much preferred over a negative response (such as telling me to butt out or rolling their eyes).

Being a *content-neutral* facilitator is similar to being a conductor for an orchestra. The legendary Arturo Toscanini conducted symphonies all over the world. He directed the flow of music, just as a facilitator directs the flow of conversation. However, Mr. Toscanini never played an instrument as he conducted, just as a facilitator should never state a personal opinion while facilitating.

The second competency is *facilitating the discussion*. There is nothing worse than asking a question and getting silent stares from the group. The opposite response can also occur. This is known as sheer pandemonium. You ask a question and everyone talks at once. You will learn techniques for making it easy for group members to participate and keep an orderly discussion. When this is done effectively, people will realize they can make a contribution and will be more encouraged to participate.

Effective Discussion

Betty Bogusch, Ph.D., Senior Training Analyst for Southern Company Services, must be able to conduct an effective discussion in a variety of group situations, whether the group is quiet, vocal, or a combination of both.

I do whatever it takes to get my groups involved. I help them find commonality with the use of icebreakers. This usually makes them more comfortable stating their views. I also make a point of talking to quiet people during breaks and asking specific people to present relevant topics at the next session, or next day. It's important to open up the discussion to everyone, not just to the one or two vocal individuals.

The third competency is *applying the bird's-eye view*, which means observing what is happening with the group and determining how well the members are working together. A good facilitator also constantly assesses his or her own effectiveness. Is the group on schedule and focused on the current agenda item? The group needs an objective person to point out what is happening. You will learn specific ways to identify what is happening and what to say to keep the group aware of what is happening.

What Are Icebreakers?

They are short activities done at the beginning of the meeting to get everyone relaxed and engaged. There are many books on the market that give icebreaker ideas, but here are a few samples:

- ▶ As part of an introduction, ask people to tell "something interesting" about themselves.
- ▶ Give each participant an adhesive name badge with the name of a famous person. Have each stick his or her badge on the back of someone in the room so that everyone has been labeled. Then each person has to figure out the identity of the person named on his or her badge. To do this, each person may ask only questions with yes or no answers.
- ▶ Do a human scavenger hunt by supplying each participant with a handout that contains human characteristics, such as "wearing red," "born in July," "owns five pets," "lives on the water," etc. Direct the participants to find one person in the room for each of the human characteristics.

The last competency is *managing conflict*. The focus is on managing conflict, not eliminating conflict. The facilitator is there to help people express their views openly and honestly. This can help increase the group's commitment to a particular decision because it gives people a chance to discuss their ideas. You will learn to encourage disagreement so the group can address all concerns and effectively make decisions that everyone can support.

This book begins with the more basic concepts first. Chapter 1 concentrates on the actions necessary to manage the meeting. It describes how to prepare for a meeting, including how to set goals and the proper way to develop agendas. Chapter 1 also describes how to open and close a meeting.

Chapters 2-5 concentrate on important skills for managing the group.

Chapter 2 focuses on the importance of neutrality and gives specific examples of *content-neutral* behavior. Chapter 3 teaches you how to effectively facilitate the discussion to get equal involvement from all group members. Chapter 4 discusses how well the group members are working together and ways to communicate your observations. Chapter 5 explains how to effectively manage conflict and help the members reach agreement even when they have reached an impasse.

Chapter 6 focuses on the two types of decisions groups work on—*business problems* and *business opportunities*. You will learn a method that will help structure your group's approach toward either *solving a problem* or *addressing an opportunity*. You will also learn about *root cause analysis* in this chapter.

Chapter 7 discusses meeting technology. You'll find out options for the different ways to conduct a meeting using the latest technology.

Chapter 8 describes how you can positively influence meetings as a participant. You will look at the importance of taking a risk and speaking out. This chapter also examines situations that may require your feedback and appropriate ways to give it to make meetings more effective.

Chapter 9 and Appendix A will help you apply the concepts in this book. Chapter 9 gives a series of difficult situations in which you will identify appropriate facilitator responses and then check your answers against the book's answers. Appendix A takes you through a case situation, in which you will see the concepts of this book applied to a fictitious organization. Appendix B provides some templates and tools for conducting meetings.

All you have to do is study each chapter and apply its information to your meeting. You will learn the principles taught in this book by taking the time to understand what is being discussed and doing the exercises at the end. You will find encouragement for those skills you are already practicing. Ultimately, your organization will win and so will you, personally.

You *can* break the pattern of ineffective meetings in your organization. You'll stop hearing people say, "Not another meeting!" and you'll start hearing, "What a great meeting! We were so productive!" You will contribute significantly to your organization and, ultimately, your own career.

—Frances Micale

Acknowledgments

I sincerely thank the following people for taking the time to read and make suggestions:

Betty Bogusch	Robbie Roberson
Noel Burt	Cynthia Russell
George Dahlberg	Beth Schumaker
Pete Land	Rich St. Dennis
Chuck Meeks	John Steed
Albert Micale	Sandy Stewart
Michael Micale	Heribert Stumpf
Bruce Nichols	Nicholas Tate
Deborah Peters	Gary Wetherbee

A special thanks to Jerry Reynolds, my friend and mentor, who will always be with us in spirit.

I would also like to thank Entrepreneur Press and Jere Calmes, for help and support in producing a quality product.

Chapter 1

Not Another Meeting!

Gina, a call center manager, sits at her desk, wondering how she got herself into the mess she's in. She is being given *more* things to do. She is now in charge of the staff meetings and she's got one coming up this week. Everyone hates these meetings, and now she is under the gun to "make them more productive," as her boss puts it.

Her fellow call center managers are really going to groan when she tells them about the upcoming meeting. It's a busy time of year, but excessive billing errors have occurred in the last three months. They are 20 percent higher than normal and, in addition, customer service reps (CSRs) are receiving increased customer complaints. Gina knows that when she presents this information to the other managers they'll realize the importance of the meeting and respond accordingly. After all, they *are* the call center managers. Each manager supervises 20 CSRs. Any opportunity to reduce billing errors would certainly make their jobs easier.

Her boss, John Hegate, has asked the group to identify possible causes of the billing errors. Since the managers are so busy with their regular responsibilities, he has agreed to take the appropriate steps to fix the problems the group identifies.

Although she is pressed for time, Gina is confident she can organize and conduct the meeting. She knows the appropriate process to follow and a few simple practices that can significantly improve her meeting.

This chapter will show you how Gina conducts a well-organized meeting by preparing the meeting objective and developing an agenda. You will also get tips on how to make your meetings more productive by effectively beginning a meeting, closing a meeting, and keeping the group closely aligned with the meeting agenda.

Ensuring a Meeting Is Needed

Before the next meeting is scheduled, Gina has to make sure a meeting is warranted to fulfill the objective. The last time she was asked to hold a meeting, she decided against it. That was when John wanted the call center managers to decide on a new copy machine. She had already discussed each person's preferences and most of the managers were in agreement. She sent out an e-mail to all of them to confirm their individual choices, which eliminated the need for a meeting.

The upcoming meeting is being scheduled to identify the potential causes of billing errors. She considers alternatives to holding a meeting, such as getting ideas via e-mail and using memos and phone calls. The disadvantage to these alternatives is that the managers would not be able to discuss these billing errors with each other in person. A live discussion might generate greater understanding and some additional possible causes of the problem.

Another alternative might be a brief one-on-one discussion between Gina and each group member. However, this might prove to be time-consuming. In addition, this alternative is more suited to a situation in which the subject is confidential or sensitive. The issue of billing errors needs to be discussed openly and honestly. Also, the one-on-one approach has the potential risk of making people feel they are being singled out for blame; the group as a whole should take ownership of the problem.

One other alternative to holding a meeting would be a brief stand-up discussion. Gina reasons that this could be effective if the meeting objective can realistically be achieved in 15 minutes or less. Discussing billing error causes will take longer, probably 45 minutes. Standing up for that length of time might be distracting and annoying for the group members.

However, she realizes that meetings can be expensive. She can calculate the meeting's average cost by multiplying the group's average hourly wage times the number of meeting participants times the estimated amount of time the meeting will last. These are her calculations:

$30.00 (average hourly wage) x 8 group members = $240

$240 x .75 (3/4 of an hour stated as a decimal) = $180 (cost of meeting)

A meeting would cost $180 in lost time. Also, while people are in a meeting, they can't perform work-related duties. Thus, the group's loss of productivity is also considered. There may be other costs involved, such as renting a room for the meeting and any refreshments and supplies needed.

In addition, she weighs the meeting's cost against what is to be gained from conducting the meeting: a first step in eliminating billing errors and customer dissatisfaction. Gina realizes that billing errors have the potential to alienate and drive some customers away. There would be a decrease in productivity when a CSR has to spend time correcting an error because the bill was not done right. All of these issues impact the company's business objectives. This meeting is obviously well worth the investment.

Companies Invest in Meeting Quality

Last year alone, Micale Training Corporation trained over 1000 business professionals on effective meeting management skills. Companies are willing to make this investment because meeting quality and productivity impact organizational performance.

Preparing for the Meeting

Gina knows that many meetings either succeed or fail before they ever take place, based upon what happens during the preparation phase. Her preparation will take approximately 30 minutes.

First, she will need to identify the objective for the meeting and create a statement that clearly describes what the group will accomplish by the end. This is called the *meeting outcome statement*. It is a statement of purpose that describes what the group must achieve. It identifies a concrete, specific, and tangible outcome, such as arriving at a decision, developing a solution, creating a list, or designing a plan.

The meeting outcome statement should be presented every time there is a meeting, to clarify the purpose of the gathering. It should be written before the meeting begins, posted during the meeting, and constantly referred to throughout the session.

> ## The Importance of an Outcome
>
> A meeting without an objective is like walking around blindfolded. If you don't know where you're going, you don't go anywhere. And many meetings end up that way. There's no purpose; therefore it's impossible to focus on any one subject. People leave the meeting wondering why it was scheduled.

A meeting outcome statement should be clear and it should hold the group accountable for reaching an objective.

A meeting outcome statement should be clear and it should hold the group accountable for reaching an objective. To accomplish this, always write the outcome statement as if the desired result had already been achieved. Do this by first identifying the actual result that will be reached by the end of the meeting. Place this at the top of the statement. Figure 1-1 contains a list of results meetings commonly achieve.

After identifying the desired result, write a brief description to clarify it.

For example, imagine the group is being asked to choose 20 books to purchase for the company library. First, examine Figure 1-1 and choose the result that most closely describes what the group will achieve. They are going to have to build a list of book titles, so the outcome statement should begin with "A list ...." A description of the type of list should come next.

> ## Several Outcomes
>
> A single meeting can target more than one goal. However, avoid doing too much in a limited amount of time. It may be better to schedule two meetings instead of trying to squeeze too much into one meeting.

> ## Figure 1-1. Results Used in Meeting Outcome Statements
>
> | | |
> |---|---|
> | ▶ List | ▶ Flowchart |
> | ▶ Solution | ▶ Goal Statement |
> | ▶ Decision | ▶ Survey |
> | ▶ Plan | ▶ Presentation |

The Information-Sharing Meeting

An outcome is still appropriate even if you are meeting to share information. You won't end up with as tangible a result, so consider beginning it with "A presentation on …" or "An understanding of …." For example, an outcome for a staff meeting might be "An understanding of current departmental events."

The following outcome statement accurately reflects what the meeting should accomplish.

A list of 20 book titles for the company library.

This statement makes it clear that the group will decide which books will be in the library. It will also be easy to tell whether the intended outcome was accomplished by the end of the meeting. The group will either have a list of 20 books or not.

Here is another example. A group is selecting an equipment vendor from two submitted proposals. Everyone has read the proposals and met with the vendors. The group must reach an agreement on which vendor will be maintaining and repairing equipment. First, choose the result in Figure 1-1 that best describes what needs to be accomplished during the meeting. In this case, the word "decision" is the most accurate description of what will occur. Next, provide a description of the type of decision that will be made. Here is a good meeting outcome statement for this situation:

A decision on an equipment vendor for maintenance and repair.

Another example involves plant employees who must develop a schedule to keep the plant running during outages caused by bad weather or other unexpected circumstances. The most descriptive result in this situation is a plan. Here is the outcome statement.

A plan for maintaining plant operations during outages.

When the above meeting is held, all of the participants will clearly understand what they are to accomplish and how much they will need to get done within the time frame of the meeting.

Gina considers her upcoming meeting and what is to be achieved.

Writing the Outcome

Make your outcome statements brief and to the point. Take out all unnecessary words. This will make your statements commonly understood by all participants.

Deciding on the Type of Meeting

Once you've written your outcome, you can identify the type of meeting: information sharing or decision making. This will determine your role (director for sharing information or facilitator for making a decision). It will also determine the role of meeting participants (listening and asking questions for sharing information or contributing ideas and deciding for making a decision). You will communicate these roles when you kick off your meeting, as explained later in this chapter.

The call center managers must identify what is causing the billing errors that customers have been complaining about. The most appropriate result is a list. Gina adds a phrase that describes the list.

A list of possible causes of billing errors experienced by customers.

This intended outcome accurately reflects what the group is expected to accomplish by the end of the meeting. It also makes it easier for Gina to take the next step, which is writing the agenda for the meeting. The *meeting agenda* is the "road map" used by the facilitator to chart the steps the group will follow to achieve the intended outcome for the session.

The agenda should be posted and referred to during the meeting. It can also be sent out ahead of time.

Using Maps

My husband Jim and I love to take excursions on our boat in beautiful Perdido Bay in Orange Beach, Alabama. Jim drives the boat and I help him navigate. If we have a certain destination (intended outcome) in mind, we follow a map (agenda) very closely so we will reach it within an acceptable amount of time. If we don't have a particular destination in mind, we take the scenic route.

It's the same for meetings. If an outcome hasn't been identified, groups are often unable to make progress. They easily get off track or become confused about what is going on. Also, if they do not use an agenda, they will not have anything to guide them toward their intended outcome. Both an outcome and an agenda are needed to get the group where it wants to go. A meeting should never be like a scenic boat excursion.

The agenda should be posted and referred to during the meeting. It can also be sent out ahead of time. You may choose to develop a detailed agenda for your own personal use (such as the one in Figure 1-2) and create a less detailed agenda for the participants.

Figure 1-2. Example of a Meeting Agenda

Meeting Agenda

Expected Outcome: A list of possible causes of billing errors experienced by customers
Date: March 3rd
Time: 2:00 p.m.
Place: Conference room, 2nd floor
Who Should Attend: J. Loom, J. Caravell, F. Black, C. Douglas, B. Williams, L. Gunther, J. Hegate, A. Toll, L. Tomas, J. Towey

WHAT	TIME	WHO
Beginning of the Meeting		
Welcome the group	30 seconds	John Hegate
Clarify the outcome	3 minutes	
Set role expectations	1 minute	
Establish ground rules	30 seconds	
Discuss agenda	30 seconds	
Body of the Meeting		
Brainstorm possible causes	18 minutes	
Clarify causes	10 minutes	
Eliminate unnecessary causes	10 minutes	
End of the Meeting		
Summarize against outcome	30 seconds	
Verify action items	30 seconds	
Praise the group's effort	30 seconds	

When you develop a detailed agenda, begin with writing down the intended outcome, the time scheduled for the meeting, the place, and who will be attending the meeting. This is shown in the top section of Figure 1-2. Also shown here is the list of meeting participants. Limit the number of meeting participants to those who will contribute information or those who will be impacted by what is discussed in the meeting. If appropriate, also invite people who can give needed support. If a key person can be present for only part of the meeting, organize the agenda topics around the time that person is present.

The meeting agenda is divided into three columns—What, Time, and Who. "What" is the topic to be discussed or the activity. "Time" is the estimate of how much time will be needed for each agenda item. The "Who" column is used to note the names of guest speakers or to indicate that some-one other than the facilitator will be making a presentation. The agenda in Figure 1-2 indicates that John Hegate will be a guest speaker. He is only there to answer questions about the problem. He is the one who initiated this improvement effort, so he wants to make sure the managers understand what is expected. After he answers their questions, he will leave so that they can work without any interference from him.

Concentrate on the "What" column first, because this is where you iden-tify actions needed to progress toward the intended outcome. In Figure 1-2 there are five easy steps listed under "Beginning of the Meeting." They describe the steps a facilitator takes to open a meeting. Use these same steps for every meeting you kick off.

Steps covered in the body of a meeting agenda differ from one meeting to the next, because the intended outcome is usually different.

Using Verbs

The "What" column shows action, so always begin each agenda item with a verb; this ensures clarity.

Steps covered in the body of a meeting agenda differ from one meeting to the next, because the intended outcome is usually differ-ent. Develop this area with your meeting outcome statement in mind. Ask yourself what the group must do to reach the intended outcome. List the steps needed to accomplish this.

For example, Gina's intended outcome is a list of possible causes of billing errors. She reasons that the group will most likely brainstorm all the causes they have observed and have learned about through the CSRs' comments and customer complaints. She also knows John Hegate will use this list to see which causes occur most often. The list might need clarification, so that John understands each cause completely.

Gina decides to begin with asking the group to *brainstorm* a list of billing error causes. Brainstorming occurs when people give ideas on a par-ticular subject without deciding if the idea is a good one or a bad one. The list may end up with some causes the group decides to remove later. However, brainstorming will ensure that none of the important causes are left out. Gina assigns a time of 18 minutes, because the list will be lengthy.

As shown in Figure 1-2, the next step after brainstorming is to *clarify* the list of causes. Clarifying means explaining the meaning of an item on the list. Gina will make sure that any item not understood by a participant is explained by the participant who originated it. She assigns 10 minutes to this agenda item.

The next step is to *eliminate* any unnecessary causes on the list. This is possible only after the participants understand the items through clarification. Gina will ask them if any causes that aren't realistic can be deleted from the list. She estimates 10 minutes for discussion.

Once you have filled in the items for the body of the meeting, it is time to complete the agenda by adding the end of the meeting items. The three steps listed are the same ones used for all meetings: summarize, verify action items (or commitments made during the course of the meeting), and praise the group for a job well done.

Figure 1-3 lists meeting preparation questions that help you identify the meeting outcome, agenda, people to invite, and other important elements. The Meeting Preparation to-Do List (Figure 1-4) includes all the key actions that must take place in the preparation phase. Once you've developed the meeting outcome and agenda, you're ready to send an announcement informing those who are invited. In addition, you'll need to schedule the room and refreshments. This list can help you handle these arrangements without leaving anything out.

Once you have filled in the items for the body of the meeting, it is time to complete the agenda by adding the end of the meeting items.

Figure 1-3. Meeting Preparation Questions

1. What do you want to happen as a result of this meeting?
2. Is there an alternative to holding this meeting?
3. Who expects to be involved and wants to attend?
4. Who could contribute something and needs to attend?
5. Who needs information both beforehand and afterwards?
6. What topics need to be covered that support the desired result?
7. How long will it take to discuss each topic?
8. What are the estimated length, place, and time for the meeting?
9. What information should be sent out in advance?
10. What other preparation do participants need in advance?
11. What equipment is needed?
12. How should the room be arranged?
13. Who is leading or facilitating the meeting?
14. What other roles are needed and who will fill them?

Figure 1-4. Meeting Preparation to-Do List

1. Identify problem/need/expectation.
2. Develop a meeting outcome.
3. Develop the agenda.
4. Send out announcement of meeting.
5. Book room, refreshments, and audiovisuals.

Planning for Group Reaction

If you know that a meeting that you'll be conducting will cause the participants to react negatively, plan for it. Anticipate what that negative response might be and develop some strategies for dealing with it. For example, if a new reorganization won't be well received by the group, decide on what you'll say to address their concerns.

Beginning of the Meeting

There have been numerous occasions when group members have approached me at a break and said, "I am getting a lot out of this meeting. That doesn't surprise me because you started out very effectively."

Beginning a meeting effectively and thoroughly is not difficult; you just have to guide the group through five steps.

Beginning a meeting effectively and thoroughly is not difficult; you just have to guide the group through five steps. These steps may be covered in depth or very quickly, depending upon how formal the meeting is and how often the participants have met together in the past. If the group knows the routine, go through them quickly without compromising a clear understanding of what is going to happen.

At the beginning of the meeting, welcome the group and create a positive tone. To do this:

▶ Make any necessary introductions if any participants don't know each other.

▶ Make sure the participants know the location of restrooms and phones.

▶ Announce when the meeting will end and cover other logistical issues.

▶ Refer to any action items that should have taken place at a previous meeting.

Next, clarify the intended outcome for the meeting as follows:

Proper Welcome

A proper welcome will set a positive tone for the rest of the meeting. Participants who sense that you are organized and in control will place more importance on the time that is being spent for the meeting.

Of course, this includes starting the meeting on time and ending it on time. By beginning a meeting at the scheduled time, you will go very far in establishing credibility with the participants. The participants should trust that you will also end it on time and so be willing to give their full attention to the meeting topics, as opposed to wondering when the meeting will end! Then, end the meeting on time. Time is precious to all. Respect it.

▶ Read the posted outcome for the group.

▶ Describe any parameters surrounding the outcome and provide any useful background information. *Parameters* are limits for the group, including deadlines, budget constraints, or consequences of the project at hand.

▶ Ask for questions to ensure that the participants understand the intended outcome.

▶ Refer to the intended outcome as the meeting progresses, to keep the group focused.

▶ Summarize which phase the group is currently focusing on if the meeting is part of an ongoing project.

Once the meeting outcome is clarified, the group should have no question about why they are present or what has to be accomplished.

Setting role expectations is the next step for beginning a meeting. You do this so that all participants know what they are supposed to do to make the meeting a success. Start out with your role.

If you are facilitating (for a decision-making meeting):

My name is _____ and I'm going to be your facilitator today. I will help you work toward your intended outcome by helping you create a list of the causes of billing errors. I'll make suggestions to help you get there faster, but I won't contribute my opinion on what you should do to reach the outcome. If you find that I am too involved and am getting in the way, please let me know.

If you are directing (for an information-sharing meeting):

Clarifying the Outcome

You will clarify your meeting outcome most effectively by posting it on a wall before the meeting begins. When it is time to present it to the group, walk over to it, and point to it while you read it aloud. These simple actions will ensure that everyone understands why the meeting was scheduled.

Setting role expectations is the next step for beginning a meeting. You do this so that all participants know what they are supposed to do to make the meeting a success.

My name is _____ and I'll be conducting today's meeting. I will be sharing some information with you. If you have questions at any time, please feel free to ask. If I don't know the answer, I'll find out and get back to you.

Of course, in most instances, the participants will already know you, so you won't need to be so formal. But it is most important that they comprehend your role when you are facilitating, since this role can be misunderstood.

The participants also need to understand their role. Are they supposed to share their ideas? Are they supposed to make a decision? Or are they only expected to listen and ask questions about a decision that's already been made? The posted outcome statement will partially communicate what the group is expected to do. But they also need to know whether this meeting is for sharing information or making a decision.

If they are there to share information, then their role is to simply listen and ask clarifying questions. But if the meeting is to make a decision, then participants will be expected to contribute ideas and become much more involved. Figure 1-5 gives you more information about this. Make sure you accurately communicate your own role in leading the meeting (director or facilitator) and the meeting participants' roles (receiving information or making a decision).

Handling Latecomers

Expect that some people will arrive late. If you can quickly tell them what has happened so far, do so immediately. If the latecomer has missed too much of the meeting, offer to give a synopsis at the next break or at the end of the meeting.

Figure 1-5. Participant Roles by Type of Meeting

Participant Roles	Information Sharing	Decision Making
Meeting Leader	(such as staff meetings, announcing a new policy or procedure, presenting any other information—director)	(such as solving a problem, creating a plan to implement a decision, addressing a business situation—facilitator)
Meeting Participant	Receiver of Information	Decision Maker or Contributor of Ideas

Assigning Special Roles

Avoid calling on people to take on certain roles. Asking for volunteers is much more effective and the comfort level of the person volunteering will be higher. Once you have the volunteers you need, give each person a quick explanation of how to effectively carry out his or her duties.

There are other roles that you might want to fill during the meeting, depending upon the meeting outcome. They are listed below.

Recorder:	Normally, the facilitator records ideas on an easel. If the group is very large (more than 15 participants) or if the facilitator prefers, one person can serve as recorder and concentrate on *boarding* ideas so the facilitator can focus on conducting the discussion. Boarding ideas means writing down the ideas on a flip chart for everyone to view.
Timekeeper:	The timekeeper keeps track of time during the meeting. This is important because it prevents the group from spending too much time on an issue and ending the meeting without reaching the outcome. A good timekeeper periodically points out how the group's progress compares with the time allotted for each agenda item.

Co-facilitator:	When there are more than 15 participants, two people can take turns facilitating. While one facilitator is conducting the meeting, the other can help keep the group focused by quietly breaking up side conversations.
Coordinator:	The coordinator handles meeting logistics, such as booking the meeting room, sending out memos announcing the time and place, and handling the refreshments for breaks and lunch.
Minutes taker:	The traditional duty of the minutes taker is to write down a summary of decisions made. This could include writing down the flip chart notes that are boarded by the facilitator or recorder. If the group is discussing a lot of detailed information that must be passed on to people outside the meeting, asking for someone to take detailed discussion notes might also be helpful.

Managing Special Meeting Roles

It is important to manage the people who volunteer for additional roles. For example, if you choose to have someone record group ideas while you facilitate the discussion, make sure the recorder accurately captures all ideas contributed. If the recorder gets too involved in the discussion by asking questions and taking on your facilitator role, call a break and remind him or her to stick to recording only. This will prevent confusion over who is leading the meeting.

Ground rules are established to help meeting participants work together more effectively.

Ground rules are established to help meeting participants work together more effectively. You may present your own ground rules ahead of time or, time permitting, ask the group to develop its own. Develop ground rules to specify behaviors that will help make the meeting more successful, such as:

▶ Be on time.

▶ Avoid interrupting others.

▶ Participate!

▶ Respect the opinions of others.

Creating Their Own Ground Rules

If there is time, have the participants create their own ground rules. This will generate a high level of commitment. Consider using a tool called a *contingency diagram*.

First, ask them to suggest all the actions they could take that would make the meeting unproductive or ineffective. Board their ideas on the flip chart. Then ask them to suggest what the opposite of each action would be. For example, "not participate" would become "participate." The final list would become the group's ground rules.

▶ Do not engage in personal attacks.

If the same group meets regularly, at the beginning of each session refer quickly to the ground rules that were previously developed. After presenting the ground rules, secure the group's commitment to following them. This is called *contracting* with the group, as in this example:

These are our ground rules. Do I have everyone's commitment that you will follow these guidelines?

If members agree to follow the ground rules, it is easier to enforce them should the need arise. If members don't agree with the ground rules, ask them to make whatever changes are necessary so they *can* commit to them.

Ground Rules That Work

When presenting and contracting an already established list of ground rules, use caution. Avoid talking down to the participants by presenting the rules diplomatically. Say, "These guidelines have helped other meetings become more productive. If you like the idea, we could use them in our meetings." The participants must make the final decision on whether ground rules are used and which ones are included.

The last step for beginning a meeting is to present the agenda. Briefly review the agenda and ask if there are any questions or points that need clarification. This will show the participants what has to happen in order to reach the outcome. The agenda should be posted or handed out and referred to throughout the meeting.

Body of the Meeting

After you cover the agenda, you have completed the five steps for beginning the meeting. That sets the stage for the real work, the body of the meeting. This work becomes the middle of your agenda, as shown in Figure 1-2.

Make sure every-one knows what the group is doing by periodi-cally pointing to the current agenda step.

Your main task is to guide the group through each agenda step. Make sure everyone knows what the group is doing by periodically pointing to the current agenda step. Don't lead the group to the next step until making sure everyone is ready to move on. This is called reaching closure. Ask the group, "Is everyone ready to move on to the next step?"

When the group is considering different options, you may need to board their ideas on a white board or flip chart. If possible, use a flip chart. This adaptable tool allows you to board ideas and post them, so that the ideas remain in front of the participants for review. You can use color to make your chart easier to read. I suggest alternating between two colors. Just remember to write large enough for everyone to see—at least one and a half inches tall.

During the discussion, participants may point out action items that are needed. When this happens, make a note of each one, along with who will be responsible for it and when it will be completed. Verify this information at the end of the meeting so that everyone will be aware of commitments made.

End of the Meeting

The way a meeting ends sets the tone for implementing the decisions made. If the group did not achieve the goal specified in its outcome statement, the members can decide to extend the meeting or schedule another one. This is a group decision, since it is your responsibility to end the meeting on time. Only the group members can take responsibility for extending the planned ending time.

When the group is satisfied that it has achieved the intended outcome, you are ready for the first step needed to end a meeting, called summarizing. Discuss what was accomplished or decided during the session and revisit any unfinished business.

- ▶ Reiterate any decisions made or any progress toward the outcome.
- ▶ Discuss any issues that have not yet been resolved; ask the group members how they want to handle these issues.
- ▶ Set the date, time, and place for the next meeting.

To verify action items at the end of a meeting, refer to the list you've been keeping. Make a point of noting all commitments made by group members and any action items that have been established. Then, as the meeting wraps up, verify who will do what and by what date the task will be completed. These action items should also be revisited at the next meeting, if appropriate.

Make a point of noting all commitments made by group members and any action items that have been established.

Another important step for ending a meeting is to praise or thank the participants for a job well done. This will help end the meeting on a positive note. Of course, do it with sincerity. Try to identify specific ways they worked together effectively, achieved their intended outcome within the time limits, listened well, or persisted through a challenging process.

After the Meeting

What you do after the meeting is as important as what you do during the meeting. You may need to check with group members who volunteer to accomplish agreed-upon tasks. If there was a request for additional information during the meeting, you may be the person responsible for getting the information and communicating it back to the group. You also need to notify the appropriate people of any decisions made during the meeting.

Publishing meeting results is an important part of follow-up. Shortly after the meeting, write up a brief summary of the meeting highlights. Point out what progress was made toward the designated outcome. Include the action items that were set, the participant who is responsible for each action, and by what date the action should be completed. If there are any misunderstandings, individual participants can then contact you in order to clarify their roles or their understanding of the meeting outcome.

Another important follow-up activity is to evaluate the meeting's effectiveness. Obtaining feedback about your skill in facilitating the meeting is important.

First, complete a self-evaluation of your handling of this meeting. Figure 1-6 can be used for this purpose. Review this checklist of the steps for facilitating a meeting effectively. Evaluate your role in completing each of the steps. Think through the facilitation skills. List any unanticipated problems that occurred. Which ones did you handle particularly well? Congratulate yourself on your efforts. Then choose one skill area where you think you could improve. Decide what you need to do to improve this skill the next time.

Figure 1-6. Self-Evaluation Form

Meeting Facilitation Self-Evaluation Form

Ensuring a Meeting Is Needed
____ Did I determine the purpose for the meeting?
____ Did I compare alternative methods for fulfilling the purpose?
____ Did I evaluate the cost for the meeting?
____ Did I consider business objectives in deciding whether or not to call a meeting?

Preparing for the Meeting
____ Did I write a meeting outcome statement?
____ Did I invite the right people?
____ Did I decide on the meeting time?
____ Did I choose the location (and reserve the space, if necessary)?
____ Did I write the meeting agenda?
____ Did I create and distribute the agenda?

Beginning of the Meeting
____ Did I welcome the participants?
____ Did I clarify the meeting outcome?
____ Did I discuss any roles needed?
____ Did I establish ground rules?
____ Did I discuss the agenda?

Body of the Meeting
____ Did I lead the group through the planned agenda?
Did I successfully handle the discussion by:
____ using active listening?
____ using questions effectively?
____ directing the conversational flow so all participated?
____ displaying tact?
____ letting the group make the decisions?
____ Did I keep the meeting on track?

End of the Meeting
___ Did I summarize progress toward the meeting outcome?
___ Did I verify action items?
___ Did I congratulate group members on efforts and accomplishments?

Follow-up
___ Did I follow up on action items?
___ Did I obtain feedback on meeting facilitation skills?
___ Did I use the feedback to improve my meeting facilitation skills?

Obtain feedback from the participants. Either ask them personally what you did well and how you need to improve or request that they give you written feedback, either in a memo or through e-mail.

Use the feedback to continuously improve your facilitation skills. You'll be amazed at the improvement in productivity and reduced participant frustration that result from using your new meeting facilitation skills.

What Is Feedback?

Feedback is a gift from someone who objectively sees your performance. But you have to consider the source. Take all feedback you receive into consideration and use what you feel is most relevant. Be willing and open to making changes.

Chapter Summary:
A Prescription for Better Meetings

The techniques in this chapter are fundamental to ensuring that your meetings are structured to *get something done*!

Ensuring a Meeting Is Needed

Review alternatives, such as using e-mail, making phone calls, conducting one-on-one discussions, or having brief stand-up meetings. Consider the actual cost of the meeting that is planned.

Preparing for the Meeting

Ask yourself the following questions:

▶ Has a meeting outcome statement been developed?

> ▶ Has an agenda been developed?
> ▶ Have the right people been invited?

The Beginning of the Meeting

Use the following steps to kick off a meeting:

> ▶ Welcome the participants, make necessary introductions, and check the status of action items from previous meetings.
> ▶ Clarify the meeting outcome.
> ▶ Set role expectations.
> ▶ Contract the ground rules.
> ▶ Present and describe the meeting agenda items, so the participants know what will be happening during the session.

The Body of the Meeting

The body of the meeting is where the actual work toward the intended outcome takes place. Guide the group through each agenda step, one at a time.

The End of the Meeting

A good summary at the end of a session caps off what has been accomplished and verifies what the group has agreed to during the meeting.

> ▶ Point out progress against the outcome.
> ▶ Verify any action items.
> ▶ Praise the group's effort.

After the meeting is over, the work is not. Remember:

> ▶ Follow up as necessary.
> ▶ Publish the results of the meeting.
> ▶ Evaluate the meeting's effectiveness.

Practicing these fundamentals will ensure that your meetings are on track and productive. As Gina has learned, the reputation of being an effective meeting facilitator means that you will get impressive levels of attendance, full participation, and solid support for decisions made in all your meetings!

Chapter 2

I Thought I Knew How to Facilitate

Rob is a plant manager who has been assigned the facilitator's role for his departmental quarterly meeting. He's been with the company for 21 years and feels that he can make a positive contribution. The group was asked to make several decisions, but he's sure he can steer them in the right direction. He has more experience than most of the group members and they look up to him. He expects that the group will accomplish a lot if he can get them to do what he knows is best for the company.

Rob will definitely make an impact—probably the wrong one. It is clear that he intends to lead and expects the group to follow. Yet, since the whole group is charged with making the decisions and Rob has been assigned the role of facilitator, he should avoid stating his own opinions. Otherwise, group members may end up wondering why they're involved if one person is making all the decisions!

There is a common misconception about facilitation. Well-meaning individuals, like Rob, often take on the role of facilitator without really understanding what it involves. The true facilitator should be neutral on all issues and avoid giving personal opinions. If the group has been given the authority to make a decision or share input, then the person leading the meeting must facilitate and maintain neutrality.

Following the Appropriate Role

If you act like a director when the meeting situation calls for a facilitator, watch out! You might find yourself getting little commitment to the project and doing most of the work yourself.

This chapter will explore the issues around facilitator neutrality. You will learn when it's appropriate to give your opinion and when it's not. Several examples will be discussed that illustrate how to communicate clearly while focusing on how the group is working together. This information will help you facilitate with neutrality and encourage your groups to take responsibility for solving problems and addressing opportunities.

What Is a Facilitator?

A facilitator is someone who helps meeting participants work together to make decisions, develop plans, and then implement those plans.

A *facilitator* is someone who helps meeting participants work together to make decisions, develop plans, and then implement those plans. This description implies that it is the group that is responsible for the making decisions, planning, and implementing. The facilitator simply *makes it easy* for the group to carry out its function. This distinction between the facilitator and the group is important, because it clarifies the roles and responsibilities for all involved. While the facilitator is responsible for making it easy for the group to perform, the participants are responsible for their own success. The group must ultimately answer to management: What has it accomplished?

Here is an example:

Judy manages a group of 12 people in network operations. The group writes methods and procedures for the rest of the company. Members are currently revamping one of the methods, which was put into practice five years ago. They were told that their collective recommendation would be implemented.

Who Should Be a Facilitator?

Choosing a facilitator requires careful consideration. The facilitator could be anyone: the group leader, the manager, or a group member. However, the best person for the job is usually one who can take a neutral part in the group's work. It is easier to facilitate if you don't have strong opinions about the specific project the group is working on or if you are able to keep your personal opinions to yourself.

Judy has some specific ideas about how this method should be revised, so she decides to facilitate the process in order to give her input.

In this example, Judy is clearly not the best person to facilitate, because she has specific ideas about what she wants the group to accomplish. There are two problems with this. First, Judy will probably end up controlling the group's decisions, even though members will expect to have the authority to make decisions themselves. The facilitator's role inherently carries a certain amount of authority. It's easy to lead the group in a specific direction, as opposed to allowing it to find its own direction. Second, because Judy is the manager of the group, she will throw her weight around to stay in control.

The Boss as Facilitator

If you're thinking about facilitating a meeting of your direct reports, think again. It's almost impossible for a manager to avoid influencing reports when he or she asks for their input. People tend to say what they think their boss wants to hear, rather than being candid. No matter how neutral you may think you are, if the issue requires wholehearted commitment, get someone else to facilitate. Let the group work on its own, without you in the meeting. Then you can be confident that you received their honest ideas and recommendations.

A situation like this is very damaging. The group members, believing they were not allowed to do what they were initially promised, end up being at best only partially committed to the final outcome. They will wonder why they were brought together and question the manager's credibility.

There are many facilitators who have specific opinions but are able to withhold their comments. Consider Martin's situation.

Martin is a team leader responsible for facilitating a group of plant employ-ees. They are responsible for scheduling maintenance for plant equipment. Martin maintained equipment in a previous job, so he has specific ideas about how equipment should be maintained, but he realizes he will need to remain silent. Without any interference from Martin, the employees will be allowed to decide on a maintenance schedule and fully support the plan they've developed.

Martin understands the importance of letting a group take ownership for its decisions. He avoids stating his own opinion, concentrates on moving the group through the agenda, and allows the members to draw their own conclusions.

> ## Credibility: It's Crucial
>
> Credibility for a manager and a facilitator is crucial. The group must be able to trust that you will do what you say you're going to do. In today's world, credibility is a word that gets thrown around a lot. You've heard the phrase, "Walk the talk." These are overused words and sometimes detract from the real message. You can't be a strong facilitator without credibility. If you don't know the answer to something, admit it, then promise to find out the answer and communicate it. If the group members are told they will be able to make a decision themselves, let them make it.

Content vs. Process

To be an effective facilitator, you must first understand the differences between *process* and *content*. Knowing these differences will help you guide a group through the process and do the real job of a facilitator. You will also become better at staying out of the content.

To be an effective facilitator, you must first understand the differences between process *and* content.

Process refers to the way the group works together. It's the methodology the group uses. Process is *how* a group achieves a goal. As the facilitator, you develop the process for the group by identifying the meeting outcome statement and writing the agenda.

For example, imagine that a group is meeting to develop a list of materials needed for the new company library. In the group's process, the members use methods like these to help them develop an effective list.

- ▶ Brainstorm a list of desired items.
- ▶ Clarify items on the list.
- ▶ Eliminate from the list items that the group agrees are unnecessary.

There are also process issues that involve behavior. Ground rules like these suggest how the group should work together.

- ▶ Allow only one person to talk at a time.
- ▶ Be on time.
- ▶ Participate fully.

Content refers to the actual ideas, suggestions, and decisions that come out of a group discussion. Content is *what* a group does to achieve a goal.

Consider the group that is meeting to develop a list of materials needed for the new company library. In developing content, members discuss items that they'd like to have in the library. Those items include the following:

- a sofa
- two tables and eight chairs
- one bookshelf
- a desk
- a coffee machine
- a soft drink machine

Figure 2-1 gives you a summary of process and content. Process refers to elements that describe how a group will work together to reach the intended outcome. Content refers to what the group decides to do to reach an outcome.

Figure 2-1. Process vs. Content		
Process, the "How"	Content, the "What"	Content Examples
Brainstorm a list.	A specific opinion	"I prefer XYZ vendor."
Clarify a list.	A specific fact	"Our market share is 25%."
Decide by discussing pros and cons.	A specific idea	"I think we should do some benchmarking."
Eliminate items from a list.	A specific decision	"We will use a team to interview candidates."
Listen effectively.	A specific action	"We will call a sampling of customers."

Content-Neutral and Process-Oriented

The facilitator should show neutrality on all content issues through appropriate words, body language, and voice tone. Actions can be just as important as words in displaying neutrality.

The facilitator in the following examples is *not* being content-neutral:

A telecommunications company has been experiencing an unusual number of outages. A group of technical support representatives (TSRs) is meeting to determine how to reduce these service failures. Julia, one of the TSRs, makes a suggestion for Olivia, the facilitator, to write on the flip chart. Olivia doesn't agree with the suggestion. She shrugs and moves on, not adding the item to the list.

The Traffic Cop

Have you ever observed a police officer in an intersection? He or she stands in the middle of the street, telling cars when to go, stop, or turn. The officer is directing traffic, just like a facilitator directs the flow of discussion. The officer never drives anyone's car, just as the facilitator never contributes ideas to the discussion. In this way, the officer and facilitator maintain neutrality. However, the officer might show his or her disapproval of a driver's style with a scowl or frown. The facilitator *could* show the same type of disapproval. Both words and body language must be kept in check to maintain authentic neutrality.

It is not up to the facilitator to decide whether an item is worthy of consideration. The facilitator should write down all suggestions. The members of the group should be able to consider and discuss all ideas at the appropriate point in the process, regardless of what the facilitator thinks of any idea.

A group of call center managers is meeting to decide how to handle a recent increase in call volume. They report to Tony, who also happens to be the facilitator. Tony sees the group struggling at an important decision point. He finally says, "OK, everyone. We're going to do it this *way."*

The facilitator should always allow group members to make the decision, even if they have to struggle or seem uncertain. It is still the group's decision to make, even if you are both the facilitator and the boss. If they were originally given the authority to make the decision, they should be encouraged to make it.

A lumber company has been trying to increase its market share by pursuing retail businesses. The sales group has been developing a plan that lays out how retail businesses should be approached. The group reaches a consensus on the plan, but the facilitator, Vincent, does not think it will work. He says, "That's not an acceptable decision. Try something else."

The facilitator should live with the group's decision, whatever it is.

A group of attorneys is meeting to identify options for defending one of their clients. Andrea, an influential senior attorney, makes a suggestion. The facilitator, Michael, really likes this particular suggestion and says, "That's a great idea."

The facilitator should always allow group members to make the decision, even if they have to struggle or seem uncertain.

26

Let the Group Struggle

There is value in allowing everyone to struggle at important decision points. Group members will learn from the discussion, disagreement, and effort. Avoid the temptation to step in and save them from disagreeing or feeling frustrated. Unless the issue is small and your intervention could prevent them from wasting time, allow the participants to work out their ideas. This will build ownership and increase satisfaction when they achieve results.

Even if the facilitator likes an idea, he or she should make no attempts to influence the group.

The facilitator should deal only with the meeting's process issues and be *process-oriented*. In other words, focus on *how* the group is working together.

Here are some examples of what the facilitator *should* say in order to be process-oriented:

A group of programmers is meeting to decide on a new system that will be more productive and more reliable. They are very excited about the opportunity to make some significant improvements in the organization. They start making suggestions enthusiastically, but several people are talking at the same time. Tonya, the facilitator says, "It seems that there is a lot of interrupting going on. Let's remember our ground rules and have just one person talking at a time."

The facilitator is concerned with *how* the group is communicating, not the ideas being discussed. This is appropriate.

John, a service manager for a large sporting goods chain, wants to make a comment about a diagram that Mary is presenting to the group. He interrupts her and causes her to lose her train of thought. Judy, the facilitator, says, "John, could you please hold on? I'll get right back to you as soon as Mary has finished explaining this diagram."

The facilitator is acting as a conductor in directing the flow of the conversation just as a conductor directs the flow of music. This provides a needed service to the meeting-goers.

A group of supervisors has just completed brainstorming a list of possible performance standards for their telemarketing representatives. It is time for the group to clarify anything on the list that is unclear. Jason, the facilitator, asks the group, "Does anyone need clarification of these suggestions?"

The facilitator is ensuring that group members understand the ideas so that they will be able to accurately assess the ideas.

The facilitator is concerned with how the group is communicating, not the ideas being discussed.

Nonverbal Language

Be aware of your nonverbal communication: voice tone and body language. While you may not *say* anything that denotes your opinion, your nonverbal language might be communicating something. It's easy to show displeasure by scowling, shaking your head, or simply not boarding an idea that someone contributed.

Gina is facilitating the call center managers as they identify the causes of billing errors. She begins the meeting and is in the process of reviewing the planned agenda. She says, "I recommend we brainstorm a list."

Since this suggestion focuses on a process, it is appropriate for the facilitator to make a recommendation, unless the group prefers doing something else.

Matthew is facilitating a group that is brainstorming a list of solutions for improving productivity in the key entry department. The participants have been brainstorming for 20 minutes and are making fewer and fewer suggestions. Matthew says, "It seems that the flow of ideas has slowed down. Are we ready to move on to the next step?"

You've Got to Practice

People learn to be *content-neutral* only after practicing it. In my seminars on meeting management, I've found that it's easy to understand the concept mentally and more challenging to put it into practice. Give yourself permission to make mistakes and learn from them.

Remaining content-neutral means accepting group decisions, ideas, and input. Being process-oriented means concentrating on how the group is working together and the route that will be followed to reach the intended outcome.

This question keeps the group moving forward and is an appropriate statement for the facilitator to make.

Figure 2-2 describes the behaviors a facilitator exhibits for remaining content-neutral and process-oriented. This accurately describes what *should* be done to focus on the appropriate areas. Remaining content-neutral means accepting group decisions, ideas, and input. Being process-oriented means concentrating on how the group is working together and the route that will be followed to reach the intended outcome.

The Real World

Often, the appointed meeting facilitator is also directly impacted by the group's decisions. This happens because it's not realistic to bring in an outside

Figure 2-2. Examples of Content and Process	
Remaining Content-Neutral	**Being Process-Oriented**
1. Accept all ideas.	1. Encourage participation.
2. Allow the group to make decisions.	2. Ensure that all ideas and statements are heard and understood.
3. Live with all group decisions.	3. Enforce the ground rules.
4. Avoid influencing the group.	4. Focus on *how* the group is communicating.

facilitator whenever an important meeting is scheduled. When this happens, maintain your credibility as follows:

▶ Explain at the beginning of the meeting that you have a stake in the decision and would like to give your input on a limited basis. Make sure the group is comfortable with this.

▶ Acknowledge your bias by saying, "I'm stepping out of my role as facilitator to tell you that I agree with Leo's suggestion because of our deadline. Now, I'll step back into my role."

▶ Limit the number of times you give your opinion to only the most important issues. If you give your own ideas as a matter of habit, the group may start to resent your involvement and therefore resist your ideas—no matter how good.

▶ Involve yourself in the content of the meeting only to save the group unnecessary time and effort. If you know something that will help the group, share it with them: for example, "You may want to talk to Martha Porter. I believe she worked in the technology group that developed that product. She knows a lot about it."

If you have strong opinions about the issue to be discussed, it may be best to get someone else to facilitate.

If you have strong opinions about the issue to be discussed, it may be best to get someone else to facilitate. Then you can contribute as a group member and not have to worry about holding back your opinion.

Chapter Summary:
The Facilitator's Greatest Skill

This chapter discusses one of the most important skills for a facilitator. When guiding the group, you must allow participants to make their own decisions. You are there to keep them organized. They must take ownership for the business issues being addressed. By focusing on process and remaining content-neutral, you help them use their skills and experience to make a contribution to the organization.

Being Process-Oriented

Process refers to *how* the group is working together. A facilitator should be process-oriented, which means pointing out ways the participants can work together more effectively, developing the meeting outcome and agenda, and choosing methods such as brainstorming.

Being Content-Neutral

Content refers to what the group is doing—the issues being discussed or matters it must address. A facilitator should be content-neutral, which means not sharing personal opinions but instead helping the group to confer and decide. If group members have been given authority to make a decision, they resent a facilitator who forces opinions on them. They often will give up their authority and stop participating. Commitment and ownership will disappear. The facilitator's greatest skill is that of being content-neutral. It provides full support for the participants yet allows them to make the decision they feel is best. Each group member feels a greater sense of ownership and therefore takes a greater interest in making improvements in the business.

Chapter 3

How Do I Get Them to Talk?

Facilitator: "What would the group like to do with this item—delete it or keep it on the list?"
Silence.
Facilitator: "Well, what do you think?"
Still no answer.
Facilitator: "Uh, John, what do you think?"

There is nothing worse than standing up in front of a group and not getting a response to a question. It's amazing how warm the room can suddenly become when this happens. Anyone who has experienced this knows that it's uncomfortable and frustrating.

Some groups are more talkative than others. Using the right tools will help you keep quiet groups involved in the discussion and talkative groups focused on the subject. This chapter will teach you how to make this happen. Facilitating an effective discussion is possible if you utilize some important skills.

First, show you are interested in what the participants are saying by exhibiting *active listening*. This is a set of responses to encourage a speaker. (They will be discussed in detail in the next part of this chapter.) Model this skill so participants adopt it for use with each other. This will ensure good-quality communication. Second, it is important to *use questions effectively*. You will learn which types of questions encourage participation and you'll get many examples for different situations. Finally, this chapter will discuss how to direct the conversational flow so that participation is equalized among all group members, both the introverted and the extroverted.

How important is it to get wholehearted input in a discussion? As the issue being discussed becomes more serious, the need for discussion becomes more critical.

Consider the launch of the space shuttle Challenger on January 28, 1986. The mission ended 73 seconds after launch due to O-rings that did not seal in the cold temperature of 36 degrees Fahrenheit. The crew of seven, including the teacher Christa McAuliffe, perished in this tragic accident.

On the evening before the launch, managers and engineers held a telephone conference to discuss concerns about whether the launch should be delayed. Personnel from Morton Thiokol, Marshall Space Flight Center, and Kennedy Space Center were present. In her book, *The Challenger Launch Decision*, Diane Vaughan says, "worried Thiokol engineers argued against launching on the grounds that the O-rings were a threat to flight safety."

One wonders whether the phone discussion fully clarified why the engineers were concerned about the O-rings. Evidently, they were not able to convince others of the potential danger. This indicates the discussion was not as effective as it could have been. This wasn't the only factor contributing to the risks of the launch decision. But it resulted in tragic consequences.

As the facilitator, you must set the standard for effective discussion by modeling it as the group works together.

While the typical businessperson rarely makes life-and-death decisions, the need for effective discussion remains. As the facilitator, you must set the standard for effective discussion by modeling it as the group works together. By being an effective communicator, you are an example the participants will follow.

Exhibiting Active Listening

Active listening is a skill you must learn in order to be an effective facilitator. It encourages everyone to participate and ensures that each person is fully understood.

These are the three steps in the active listening process:

1. **Nonverbal acknowledgment.** This encourages the speaker to continue and assures the speaker that he is being heard. Examples are head nods, eye contact, facing the speaker, and any nonverbal cue that shows the speaker that you are paying attention to the message without taking control away from the person speaking.

2. **Rephrasing.** This is a way to verify what the speaker has said. For example, encourage reiteration by phrases such as "So, are you saying ...?" Use the rephrasing technique when the speaker is saying something that the group might not understand immediately.

3. **Empathy response.** This plays back the speaker's unspoken feelings that are expressed with voice tone and body language. It is also a very important method for showing that you have been listening and *do* understand what the speaker is trying to say. Examples of an empathy response are "You seem to be satisfied with this solution" or "I get the impression that you have some serious concerns about this option." Usually the empathy response will invite further explanation from the speaker because it encourages the speaker (and the rest of the group) to give input.

A Critical Human Need

Human beings crave the feeling of being listened to and understood. That's why prisoners of war are punished with solitary confinement. After years of isolation, only those who are mentally strong are able to return home and live normal lives once again.

Dr. Albert Mehrabian, a UCLA psychologist, conducted research on these communication elements. He found that words constitute only 7 percent of the total message. Voice tone is 38 percent of the overall message. Body language (including facial expressions and gestures) accounts for 55 percent. Since *what* a person says (the words) contributes such a small part of the total message, we are more able to understand the full essence of a message by concentrating on *how* a person is communicating (voice tone and body language).

This active listening process utilizes the three ways in which people communicate; words, voice tone, and body language.

For example, let's say your son comes home from school and says to you, "I'm not going back to school." If you are only concentrating on the words (7 percent of his message), a likely response from you would be "Oh, yes, you *are* going back to school!"

Now consider the feelings behind the words, revealed by his voice tone and body language (93 percent of the full message). Your son's downcast eyes

33

and angry voice indicate that he just had a terrible day. What would be a better response—one that would show your son you were really listening to him? Probably something like "Sounds like you had a bad day at school. What happened?" Which response would help your son be more open to a discussion with you? Definitely, the second one!

Active listening in the workplace can help you in much the same way. It gives you a better chance of really understanding a person's opinions, ideas, or concerns. In addition, people are more open to giving their input when they feel they are being heard and understood. Through active listening you create opportunities to address key issues that impact work performance.

Communicating = Listening

You can't be a great communicator without being a great listener. Impressing someone with clever language is never as effective as paying attention to the other person's perspective. By understanding others' viewpoints, you automatically win them over. It's human nature that people aren't interested in what you know until you show your interest in them.

In the early 1970s, I worked for an Atlanta-based company called Food Giant, Inc., a grocery chain consisting of 85 stores with a major share of the Atlanta market. I was asked to facilitate some of the management seminars. Most of the participants were male employees who managed the retail stores. The years of service for these managers generally ranged from 10 to 20 years. I had worked there for only a few years. It was difficult for me to "teach" these managers much of anything. They had much more experience than I did, for I was merely a recent college graduate. I quickly learned that my best chance of helping them learn the art of managing was to facilitate the discussion and listen to what they had to say. I was then able to pull together their comments and apply them to the learning points of the seminar.

To this day, I believe that I would not have been as successful in that situation if I had assumed the role of teacher, given my lack of experience. Instead, my posture was that of a good listener, which resulted in discussions that were quite valuable for everyone.

The facilitator's role includes specific active listening techniques that set the tone for meeting participants to contribute openly, just as they did at Food Giant. Here are some ways to apply active listening:

▶ Maintain eye contact with the person who is speaking. Show you are listening with head nods and other nonverbal cues.

▶ Take the input of all members seriously without discounting any suggestions: "Margaret, let's write down your suggestion so everyone can consider it."

▶ Encourage the group to address everyone's input in some way by asking for comments on a particular suggestion or by boarding the comment: "Would anyone care to comment on John's recommendation?"

▶ Periodically summarize what has been expressed by restating comments: "So far, several people have expressed their concerns about pushing back the time frame for this project."

▶ Point out the similarities among comments that have been expressed at different times: "I believe this concern was expressed earlier when Barbara was talking about the short time frame."

▶ Point out the deeper issues behind what is being expressed by observing body language and voice tone: "It seems the group is uncomfortable about the information missing from this report, but it's difficult deciding what to do about it. What ideas do you have for finding the information?"

Using Questions Effectively

Great facilitators need to be competent when asking questions. You must be able to initiate group discussions on important issues. Questions are also used to give the participants tips on how to work together more effectively. Figure 3-1 describes some common instances and sample questions that you can ask.

The following suggestions will help you generate a focused discussion. First, use open-ended questions *often*, to get at ideas, feelings, and opinions. An open question is one that requires more than two or three words to answer and more than a yes or a no. Use closed questions occasionally and only when you need to look for specific information, since they encourage specific, shorter answers.

Open: "What is your opinion of ...?"

Closed: "Does the group want to follow this suggestion?"

Open: "How would you like me to phrase that?"

Figure 3-1. Why the Facilitator Asks Questions

Reason	Example
1. To probe for specifics	"Which date in January would you prefer?"
2. To point out something you've observed	"Have we gotten off track?"
3. To reach closure and get the group's agreement to move on to a new topic	"Are we ready to move on to the next step?"
4. To get the group to participate	"What are your ideas?" or "What additional ideas do you have?"
5. To get the group's agreement	"Does everyone agree that we can remove this item from the list?"
6. To contract with the group	"Is everyone willing to follow these ground rules?"
7. To find out why the group is stuck	"We seem to be having some difficulty coming up with ideas. What's causing this?"
8. To find out feelings	"What is your feeling about this?" "Are you comfortable with this?"
9. To ensure understanding	"So, are you saying that you'd prefer a less challenging goal?"

Try This!

Here's an exercise for you to try. Seek out an acquaintance—someone you know, but not very well. Make a point of asking this person a series of open questions on any subject, personal or business. You will find that it is much easier to carry on a conversation *and* control the topics discussed, through the use of questions. The term "discussion" implies that there is more than one person speaking. To prevent a discussion from turning into a monologue (one person doing all the talking), use questions.

Closed: "Is it acceptable to say ...?"

Open: "Why do you have concerns about this opinion?"

Closed: "Are you concerned about this?"

After asking a question, allow time for the group to answer it. If you don't get an answer, try rephrasing your question to ensure that members have understood what you are asking.

> ### Expect a Delay
>
> When throwing out a question to the group, expect a five-second delay before getting a response. People have to mentally process the question, so it takes some time before they can give you an answer. Don't let this make you uncomfortable. Give the group enough time and you'll get plenty of responses.

First question: "What is your opinion of ...?"

Second question: "Are you willing to follow this suggestion?"

Note that the second question is a closed one, which is possibly another way to get participation, even if it's limited. You can always follow up with yet another question to get additional input. Just remember to ask only one question at a time, rather than throwing out two questions, one after the other, without giving the group time to answer the first one.

Ask questions that help the group take action. For example, if the members are discussing whether they want to hire outside consultants to help with a portion of the project the group is working on, here are some questions you might want to ask:

- ▶ "Who would like to explore this option further?"
- ▶ "How do the rest of you feel about this?"
- ▶ "What are the next steps you'll need to take?"

When you ask a question, accept all answers. The facilitator accepts answers 100% of the time. It is up to the group to decide the value of the input. The facilitator is there to make it easy for everyone's input to be heard and considered.

Directing the Conversational Flow

Directing the conversational flow means establishing a balance of participation among all group members. This results in a smooth flow of information passing from one group member to another. The group is then more productive and more organized in approaching its work. Directing the conversational flow effectively helps manage those individuals who tend to dominate the discussion and get more participation from those who tend to be silent.

The facilitator accepts answers 100% of the time. It is up to the group to decide the value of the input.

37

Leading Questions

Use leading questions judiciously, as they can be double-edged swords. These are questions phrased in a manner that suggests a desired answer. When such questions contain statements of opinion and begin with words like "Don't you think …?" or "Isn't it …?" they manipulate the listener into agreeing with the speaker or following the speaker's suggestions:

"Don't you think we should create a new list?"

"Isn't it going to be difficult to follow that through to completion?"

Here are some methods that will help you direct the conversational flow. First, seek equal involvement. Strive to get everyone to give input without putting anyone on the "hot seat." In other words, avoid putting someone in an awkward position by calling on him or her and expecting an immediate answer. Call on people by name only as a follow-up option. Initially, try encouraging participation from all.

Directing the conversational flow effectively helps manage those individuals who tend to dominate the discussion and get more participation from those who tend to be silent.

▶ "It's important to get as many ideas as possible. If yours is not represented on the flip chart, let us know."

▶ "Let's get everyone's input on this. Joe, have you had a chance to form an opinion at this point?"

Always discourage participants from interrupting each other. Remind them of the importance of listening to each idea, so they can understand what is being said. Furthermore, if *sidebar conversations* occur—when two or more people break off from the rest of the group for a private discussion—remind the group to listen to the person who currently has the floor.

▶ "Let's all focus on what Mary is saying."

▶ "Let's remember our ground rule of only one person talking at a time."

▶ "It's difficult for some to hear or stay focused with other discussions going on. Please hold your discussion until Maria finishes and then we'll hear from someone else."

It is critical that all members are given an opportunity to voice their ideas, suggestions and concerns. As a facilitator, you do this by acknowledging someone who is trying to give some input and promising to come back to that person at the next opportunity: "I saw Paul's hand first, but I'll come back to Richard next."

Polite Interrupting

There is one situation when *polite* interrupting is appropriate. This occurs when you are working with extremely vocal group members who contribute with a lot of detail. In this situation, it is difficult for anyone, including the facilitator, to find a break into the conversation in order to contribute to this type of discussion. In order to create an opening in the discussion for yourself or for some other eager group member, listen carefully to the person who has the floor. You can tell when this group member is about to deliver the last word of his or her message. Interrupt the last word being delivered, by saying something like "Jacob is next." This is also your opportunity to say anything that you need to say to the group.

If you have ever been hesitant to make a suggestion or comment during a meeting, then you know how important it is to give each person an opportunity to speak. The facilitator can make a difference in creating an atmosphere where it is safe for everyone to contribute.

A facilitator also needs to be proficient at writing the group's suggestions and ideas on a flip chart. Writing down ideas helps keep the flow of conversation more orderly. It isn't always necessary to log everything that is said. If you are not sure, ask the group if they are ready to list ideas and suggestions on the flip chart.

Drawing People In

The silent participants are always the toughest. It's sometimes difficult to encourage input without intimidating. Find ways to mention the person's name at relevant discussion points. For example, mention, "Joe has been observing this problem and I'm sure he will tell you what he's noticing when it's time to discuss the plan." Watch the silent person's facial expressions. You can often anticipate when they are trying to say something and want you to create an opening in the discussion.

The Flip Chart

Several types of visual aids can be used in facilitating a meeting, but the flip chart is the most useful. You can use one to build a list while the group is contributing ideas. As each sheet fills up, tear it off and hang it up with masking tape so participants can continue to refer to it. To use the flip chart effectively, keep in mind the following points:

- ▶ Make sure you have plenty of paper and different-colored markers before the meeting starts to avoid delays once the session begins.

- ▶ Use group members' exact words when boarding suggestions or ideas. If there is not enough room to use the exact words, ask the contributor of the idea, "What should I write down?"

- ▶ As you are writing down each idea, use two different-colored markers and alternate the colors. This technique makes it easier to read the ideas. Examples are blue and green or light blue and dark blue. Avoid bright colors such as red, yellow, or orange, which are more difficult to read. However, since red is emotionally charged, it can be used to highlight important areas.

- ▶ Make changes to the original list. Once a list has been built and the group is ready to eliminate or clarify items, write down the clarification next to its corresponding idea or draw a line through a discarded idea on the original list. Rewriting the list takes time and the group may become impatient.

- ▶ Keep all flip chart sheets within view of all group members for easy reference.

- ▶ Print in all lower case, except when following rules for capitalization. Capitalizing every letter makes it extremely difficult to read.

- ▶ Make your letters at least 1½ inches high so everyone can see them. Very small print is difficult for people to read.

Be Quick and Post Them

When using the flip chart, write quickly and neatly. But don't waste time making the chart overly attractive. The group will lose its momentum if you take too long to board ideas.

Post all flip charts that have the group's ideas on them. Keep several torn-off pieces of masking tape available so you can quickly grab the tape when a flip chart page is full and you need to post it on the wall.

Signs of Good Communication

Practicing these guidelines for good communication will certainly make a positive impact on how your groups interact. However, there is no guarantee that things will go smoothly.

A couple of years ago, I was facilitating a group of researchers and engineers in a large experimental facility. They were meeting to improve some of their methods and procedures. I was scheduled to spend the entire day with them, so we started the session with some icebreaker activities designed to establish rapport between the group and me.

As the morning wore on, I began to notice tension in the air. Group members were not participating. I also noticed they would not make eye contact with me. I knew there was something wrong. I tactfully mentioned that there wasn't much participation. Then I asked if there was something I could do to get them more involved. I didn't get much of a response, so I called a break and asked the same question of someone who had been more vocal during the session.

He told me that I began the session with an activity that insulted the group. (It was an evaluation process that I no longer use, as a result of this experience.) They also had some expectations that I had not bothered to investigate. I had interviewed their manager one month before but had not spoken to any group members.

Getting this feedback was not very much fun, but *not* getting it would have been even worse. At least now I could try to correct the situation. When we resumed the meeting, I apologized for my "bad start" and asked a few more questions to find out what the group needed from me. I gave them a chance to voice their concerns and used empathy, even when they gave me feedback on my own mistakes. The session turned out to be a great success, despite starting out in a ditch. Subsequently, they asked me to facilitate three additional sessions for them.

When the meeting is not going well, how can you tell? First of all, pay attention to restlessness, such as participants shifting in their seats, or becoming engaged in outside activities, such as reading or writing.

When the meeting is not going well, how can you tell? First of all, pay attention to restlessness, such as participants shifting in their seats, or becoming engaged in outside activities, such as reading or writing. The participants may need a break or something else may be bothering them. By acknowledging these symptoms early, you can change your approach.

Another sign to be aware of is when the group does not participate or when uncomfortable silences occur. This behavior is usually coupled with people avoiding eye contact with you or each other. Body language and facial expressions say a lot about how a group is feeling. This reaction can happen for a number of reasons. The group could be unhappy with you or someone else or they may not like the particular topic of discussion. First, you have to

> ### Begin with "Me"
>
> When things aren't going well, don't immediately lay the blame at the feet of an "uncooperative" or "ineffective" group. The best approach is self-examination. Ask yourself what you could be doing differently to improve the situation. Always examine your own role. Even if you didn't cause the situation, you can usually do something different to change it.

be aware if something is wrong; group members won't always tell you. After you observe it, then you can announce a break and talk to someone privately or you can tactfully ask the group as a whole what the problem is.

What are the signs a meeting is going well? You'll usually notice more excitement and enthusiasm from the partici- pants.

What are the signs a meeting is going well? You'll usually notice more excitement and enthusiasm from the participants. They are generally willing to accept input from each other and are able to interact openly to understand different perspectives. They are willing to participate and are fully engaged in the discussion. They take the time to listen and understand what is being said. There is also more tolerance for individual differences of opinion. The atmosphere is comfortable and full of energy but not tense. This is the type of meeting environment that all facilitators strive for and enjoy.

Chapter Summary:
The Importance of Communication

The manner in which we communicate with others almost always sets the tone for how others communicate back to us.

Exhibit Active Listening

Active listening occurs by observing words, voice tone, and body language. This helps ensure understanding and models how group members should be communicating with each other. Remember to maintain eye contact, take all input seriously, summarize points made during the discussion, and highlight similarities between ideas and deeper issues.

Use Questions Effectively

Effective questions help the facilitator probe for more information, point out his or her own observations, reach closure, encourage participation, verify agreement, and contract with the group. Use open questions and give the group time to answer. Remember: a facilitator accepts all answers. This practice encourages participation.

Directing the Conversational Flow

The conversation should be balanced among participants. The facilitator must seek equal involvement by discouraging interruptions, giving everyone an opportunity to speak, and writing down all suggestions on the flip chart.

The Flip Chart

The flip chart is the best tool for recording input from group members and keeping it visible throughout the meeting. Write down the exact words. When making a change, do it on the original list rather than starting a new list.

Signs of Good Communication

Be attentive to verbal and nonverbal cues to determine how the meeting is going and whether the group members are satisfied with its progress. Body language and voice tone will often indicate members' thoughts and feelings more accurately than words.

Using the principles suggested in this chapter will ensure that meeting participants are comfortable participating and have respect for each other's input. A comfortable environment makes participants more open, accepting, and willing to become fully engaged in the business of the meeting.

Chapter 4

The Art of Facilitation

Tim: "Where were we?"
Kevin: "I don't know. I lost track."
Tim: "Why can't we ever have a meeting without getting off the subject?"
Kevin: "Well, what is the subject?"

Maybe you've never expressed these sentiments, but most people have experienced them. It's challenging to encourage participation and keep everyone focused on the current topic. As a facilitator, your role is to keenly observe what is happening and make sure that the group is following the agenda. You must also monitor behavior to ensure that the members are working together as effectively as possible.

This chapter will describe how you can objectively monitor a group's progress toward its objectives. To achieve this, you must develop competencies in four areas.

The first one is *keeping the group aware*. The members need help in becoming conscious of how well they are progressing. The next competency is *building consensus*, the best method for group decision making. *Maintaining*

Getting Perspective

Have you ever parachuted from an airplane? Or seen the world from a hot air balloon? Or admired a sunset from a skyscraper? These activities give perspectives that you don't get with both feet on the ground. It is easier to notice things from an objective distance. When you are dealing with a tough issue and you go to a friend for advice, you are doing the same thing: seeking objectivity. You want to find someone to listen and respond objectively. Facilitators need to provide this as well.

---

flexibility and *displaying tact* are two other skills that reflect an awareness of the group's needs and sensitivities and a willingness to accommodate them.

To be competent in these areas, you must be able to mentally remove yourself from the situation and objectively assess what is happening among the participants. You must be able to do the following simultaneously. First, you facilitate the meeting by asking questions, listening, and leading the group through the steps in the agenda. Second, you observe how members of the group work together while constantly looking for ways they can do that more effectively. This activity is called *parallel processing*.

Keeping the Participants Aware

Keep the participants informed and aware of all pertinent information by reminding them of the desired outcome, the topics of discussion, the chosen methods for working together, and anything else that is helpful. A group can easily get off track. You can do a lot to prevent this.

Keep the group aware by being *transparent*. Candidly express your observations about what the group is doing and how members are working

---

Being a Camera

As the facilitator, you are a camera for the group. You record what you're seeing and play it back by verbalizing your observations.

Real video recording is quite valuable. I use it for a presentation skills workshop. Participants deliver their prepared presentations to the group while the camera records the speech. Then, I rewind the tape and play it back to the group. The speaker sees exactly how he or she delivered the presentation and is able to pinpoint areas of strength and areas for improvement. You can provide the same service as a VCR.

---

together. This means you'll need to monitor two main areas: what the group is working on (the tasks) and how well members are working together (the behaviors).

Constant reference to the agenda will help you concentrate on what tasks the group *should* be working on. Then you can compare this with the tasks members are *actually* working on. For example, I was recently working with a group of senior-level managers in a long-distance company. They had just brainstormed a list of solutions for improving their product rollout procedures. The agenda indicated they were supposed to be clarifying any solutions that were unclear. However, several of the managers began assessing which solutions would work and which ones wouldn't. My role, as facilitator, was to point that out by saying something like "I'm noticing that we have moved into evaluating these solutions, but we haven't finished clarifying them yet. Let's make sure we've finished the clarification process first, so that when we evaluate, we will understand what we are evaluating."

Constant reference to the agenda will help you concentrate on what tasks the group should be working on.

Always start out with a description of what is actually happening. Then explain why it is off track. It may also be helpful to describe what needs to be done to correct the situation or ask the group for their ideas. If you have observed the group doing something especially well, remember to point this out as well.

Another area to monitor is group members' behavior. This will help you focus on how well they are working together. A key area to concentrate on is whether group members are following the ground rules.

I was facilitating a group of managers who worked for a cable company. We were having ongoing meetings to improve their internal methods and procedures. One of the ground rules was to be on time. The first few times that

Enforcing Ground Rules

Once you point out that participants aren't following a ground rule, allow your group to discuss ways to encourage more effective behavior. Groups will think of ideas such as the following:

▶ Facilitator closes the door to let latecomers know the meeting has started.
▶ Participants give "thumbs up" hand signals to curtail excessive clarification.
▶ Any participant who makes a personal attack puts 25 cents into a money cup.
▶ Participants remind each other of ground rule violations.

participants came late to our meetings, I overlooked it. But I quickly realized that tardiness was becoming a pattern. To address the issue tactfully, I said, "One of our ground rules is to be on time. I'm noticing this is not always happening. What can we do to make sure people arrive on time so we can begin our meetings on schedule?" Because I pointed this out and asked for their ideas on how to correct the situation, the group was able to address it and minimize the problem.

When to Keep the Participants Aware

Here are several specific tasks and behaviors to monitor in order to keep group members aware of the following:

- ▶ Outcome
- ▶ Time frame
- ▶ Group agreements and decisions
- ▶ Group accomplishments or progress
- ▶ Current agenda item
- ▶ Group effectiveness
- ▶ Ground rules
- ▶ Parameters or background information

Outcome: When the group gets bogged down in irrelevant discussion, it can be helpful to remind them of the intended meeting outcome: "Let's remember, we have to ultimately end up with five recommendations."

Time frame: Participants can easily lose track of time. It is important that a meeting start and end on time unless the group agrees to extend it. The facilitator can issue reminders: "We have 30 minutes left. Do you want to continue clarifying these ideas or are you ready to start narrowing down the list?"

Group agreements and decisions: Remind the group of what members have already agreed upon. This helps them make future decisions: "You've already agreed to do the training in-house. What's next?"

Group accomplishments or progress: Note the progress of the group as it relates to the planned agenda or time line for its project: "We are currently on step five in the agenda and are now ready to go to step six" or "You've now established the true cause of the problem and are ready to identify possible solutions."

Current agenda item: Make the participants aware when they are discussing a topic that isn't on the agenda or is not the current agenda item: "Let's remember, we're here to discuss employee complaints, not whether we need to hire more employees. Would you like to put the subject of hiring on our *parking lot*?" A *parking lot* is a tool I use whenever I facilitate. It is a posted easel sheet entitled "Parking Lot." I use it to write down important topics that are not part of the current meeting agenda but that the group may want to address later. Make sure that all parking lot issues get addressed at some point or that there is group agreement on how those issues will be addressed.

Use the Map

Meeting participants often need prompting to stay on track. Just as you would constantly refer to a road map when you are driving to a new destination, use the agenda as a guide and refer to it often: "Now, to summarize, we're discussing ... so that we can ...."

Group effectiveness: Look for ways to compliment the group members—not on the quality of their ideas, decisions, or plans, but on their effectiveness in working together. This will help ensure your neutrality on content: "We had to work out some challenges in the beginning, but we seem to be progressing very nicely as a unified group."

Ground rules: It is sometimes necessary to remind the group of the ground rules: "One of the ground rules is to avoid interrupting one another. Even though you are enthusiastic about this issue, try to have only one person talking at a time."

Parameters or background information: There are areas not specified on the agenda that need clarification. A group operates within certain parameters such as a budget, time frame, and limits of authority. Any background information surrounding the meeting agenda is helpful: "Please, remember that we have a headcount limit of no more than five additional new hires. This was announced during the conference last month." By keeping the group aware of what's happening both inside the meeting and outside, you become a valuable asset.

Don't limit yourself to the preceding examples. These are just a few of the most important.

Consensus vs. Other Decision Making

Consensus should occur whenever the group needs commitment from all members on a particular decision or course of action. A good working definition for *consensus* is a decision made by the group that all members support. It is not necessary to have 100 percent agreement on a decision in order to have a consensus. Consensus calls for all group members to *support* the decision 100 percent, not necessarily *agree* 100 percent. It is important that group members have a clear understanding of this distinction in order to effectively reach a consensus.

There are other types of decision making in addition to consensus. They are unanimity, majority vote, and compromise.

It is almost impossible to reach a true state of *unanimity*, which means 100 percent agreement. Even after the tragic events of the attacks on the World Trade Center and the Pentagon on September 11, 2001, not all Americans agreed on the best response. Although President George W. Bush had unprecedented support, there were still some people who disagreed with his reaction to the attacks.

Relying on a *majority vote* is another pitfall for groups. People tend to resort to this easy way out when they must select one out of several choices. Someone usually says, "Let's vote on it." Voting ensures that someone loses out, with no chance to discuss his or her views. Voting tends to eliminate discussion and severely limits the level of commitment in support of the final decision. When is it appropriate to vote? When the group is considering many options (six or more) and members want to narrow the list down to a few options (two or three) for further discussion. After the list is narrowed, the group should discuss where the members stand with each option and then strive to reach a consensus.

Compromise is a settlement between two sides, each side making some sort of concession or giving up something. Compromising should also be discouraged, because it is a win-lose proposition. Each side wins something and each side also loses something. Compromise and consensus are similar, except that compromise tends to encourage limited support, since each side has to

When Stakes Are High

There are some groups that find it impossible to reach true consensus. They sometimes agree to resort to compromise, but only after every member agrees. I personally have never had to use this, but as a last resort, when the stakes are high, this might be an acceptable way to go.

give something up. On the other hand, *consensus* is a decision that each group member can fully support, because it is a win-win proposition. The decision, while not perfect for everyone, is one in which no one loses.

Here is an example that shows the difference between compromise and consensus. Most businesspeople have been involved in office moves at one time or another. This can result in major turf wars.

Imagine that your company is moving to a brand-new location in a brand-new building and will occupy the fourth and fifth floors. The fourth floor has a beautiful view and lots of windows. The fifth floor is mostly walls. Further imagine that the number of receptionists to be assigned to each department is limited. This could be the start of a long and drawn-out battle!

Of course, everyone wants to be on the fourth floor and each department needs a receptionist. But someone also has to be on the fifth floor and some departments will not receive a receptionist. An example of compromise would be if each department receives either a fourth-floor assignment *or* a receptionist, but not both. In this case, each department gains something and gives up something. There is a lot of bargaining going on.

An example of reaching a consensus is looking at it a different way, such as making the fifth-floor furnishings and decor extremely appealing, building some very nice conference rooms and break rooms, or positioning departments so that they can share receptionists. These are decisions everyone benefits from without having to give up too much.

It seems that sharing a receptionist sounds like a compromise. That may be true. Remember: consensus is similar to compromise. But if you consider what each department gets, it's clear that the consensus situation is much better for everyone than the compromise situation. Generally speaking, consensus is almost always better than compromise.

In fact, consensus is better than all other types of decision making if you want the group to make a sound decision and then support it. Consensus allows groups to hear different perspectives and points of view. By doing this, each group member is satisfied that his or her opinion was heard, even if the group chooses not to follow the course of action that he or she suggested. This creates an environment where all group members can openly discuss options and can support the group decision. People may not agree with the final decision but are willing to support it. In addition, they are typically not forced to give up something they really want. People tend to look for a way that satisfies everyone.

Consensus

When a group reaches consensus, it means that the members have discussed their issues in a safe, open environment. When participants voice their opinions in this manner, it often alters their views and makes it easier to reach agreement.

Figure 4-1 gives highlights for each type of decision making. After reviewing this chart, it will be clear how consensus works compared with the other types of decision making. Consensus is the most realistic and creates the best scenario for group members and the organization.

Figure 4-1. Types of Decision Making

	Consensus	Unanimity	Majority	Compromise
Definition	100 percent support	100 percent support	51 percent wins	Halfway point for all
Pros	All members will support	All members will support	Majority will support	All will support partially
Cons	Time-consuming	Unrealistic	Creates win-lose scenario	Creates win-lose scenario
When to use	Support is needed	Clear-cut issues	To narrow a list	Need break-through
When not to use	Short time frame	Complex issues	To make final decision	Support is needed

How to Build Consensus

Constantly look for ways to help the group reach agreement. Consensus starts with getting agreement on the ground rules at the beginning of the session. This allows the group to agree on how it will work together and sets a consensus-building precedent.

During the rest of the meeting, look for ways to continue the precedent. Keep a constant watch over each individual. Look for any signals of discomfort. Signals might include words or actions. Look for facial expressions that show confusion or concern. Watch for nonverbal signals; an individual may be hesitant without expressing it in words. If someone indicates that he or she isn't comfortable, check it out to ensure consensus: "Joan, you seem hesitant about committing to this. What do you think about this option?"

Once you've discovered that a member of the group isn't comfortable with a proposed option, help that him or her explain why to the rest of the group. Then, ask the group to develop an idea that would be acceptable to all: "So, Joan isn't comfortable with the pricing; it's too high. Has anyone else considered this?" Or "So, the pricing might be a problem. What ideas do you have that can be supported by everyone?"

When Culture Interferes

Many organizational cultures do not encourage disagreement. So your meeting participants may avoid opportunities to give their views no matter how many openings you provide for them. Your constant effort and patience will eventually draw out opposing viewpoints. If you use questions and encourage participants, it will demonstrate that you are personally comfortable with disagreement. The participants will see you as a role model and begin to open up.

If a group reaches consensus too quickly, be suspicious. Make sure that it's not because some members have decided to stop participating. If the decision is important or it has a significant impact, it would be normal for the group to struggle in its course toward consensus. You might say, "Now, I expected you to discuss this issue a little more. I want to make sure that everyone is truly comfortable with this decision. Are you?"

Encourage the group to consider all views and look for ways to reach consensus. The main function of the facilitator is to ensure that members express their opinions. This helps ensure that all members hear and understand all views: "So, Al, explain your reasons for recommending this option."

No One Method

There isn't any one method that guarantees consensus every time. You have to try different techniques and learn what fits best with your facilitative style as well as the group's decision-making style.

Ask if the group is willing to support the proposed decision or option when they are close to reaching a decision. This builds agreement and shows whether everyone is drawing the same conclusion: "Is everyone willing to support this so far?"

What to Do When the Group Gets Stuck

If the group is still struggling to reach a consensus, try some of these additional techniques. First, try encouraging conflicting factions to reverse roles. This sometimes helps people to understand opposing viewpoints: "John, if you were Mary, how would you feel? And Mary, how would you feel if you were John?"

It may be helpful to call a break. Sometimes, this helps people think about issues objectively. If people can take some time in quiet thought, the issue may not seem as serious. Often people will even use the break time to work out their differences privately.

You can help the group by reinforcing the importance of examining all sides of an issue. Remind the group that it is healthy to disagree: "It's good that we have some disagreement on this issue. It's an important issue, so we need to consider all sides." Draw out the major points of disagreement: "What specifically are you concerned about?" or "Is there something you absolutely can't live with or support?"

You can also elevate the issue. This means suggesting consideration of an outside perspective or broader issue: "What have other departments done to reinforce this training?" or "How would you advise someone to save money with their own personal income? This might help give you some ideas about the departmental budget cuts."

When to Build Consensus

A group should begin reaching consensus when smaller issues arise. This will get the members moving in an agreed-upon direction. It sets the tone and prepares them for the more important issues that they'll need to reach consensus on. You can help a group do this at several points during a meeting.

Use the flip chart to build consensus by getting everyone to agree before making changes to boarded items: "John has suggested that we remove Greenville from the list. Does everyone agree?" Any time a group member makes a suggestion to remove an item from a list, make sure the rest of the

Finding the Balance

While it's important to encourage the group to disagree, there's a balance of agreement and disagreement to strive for. Avoid pushing participants into discussing something they're not ready to talk about. No resolution will occur and you'll get the blame for it.

group is in agreement. You don't need agreement when adding an idea to a list or when clarifying an idea. However, once you begin narrowing down a list, group support is important.

Another time consensus is important is when helping a group reach closure. When working on one step of the process, ask if the group is ready to move to the next step in the process or on the agenda. "Are you ready to start evaluating these ideas? Or do you need clarification on any others?" This gives members one last opportunity to contribute to the current step in the agenda before moving on. It also points out where the group currently is according to the agenda.

When it's time to clarify the outcome and present the agenda, you help a group move toward consensus. Ask for clarification on the desired outcome at the beginning of the meeting: "What questions do you have about the outcome? Does everyone understand it?" Ensure that all members of the group understand the planned agenda, after pointing out each agenda item: "Does everyone understand this agenda?" If group members understand the result they want to achieve and how to get there by the end of the meeting, it is easier to avoid confusion and reach consensus.

Process Tools

One area in which you would not expect group agreement is on process tools. Simply recommend the ones you have selected and listed on the agenda. I have seen facilitators say, "What would you prefer doing, brainstorming or some other method?" When group members are given a choice on which methods to use, they tend to agonize over what to do. This wastes a great deal of time and group energy. There is one exception, though. If group members voice an unsolicited preference for a method you didn't plan for, be flexible to their needs.

Once the group makes a decision, always ensure that there is a true consensus. In other words, when the group makes a decision or commitment, be sure all group members can support the decision: "Is everyone willing to support this decision? John, we haven't heard from you yet—are you comfortable supporting this?" This gives all members an opportunity to voice their concerns.

Maintaining Sensitivity and Flexibility

Maintaining both sensitivity and flexibility is crucial in helping the group perform its work. *Sensitivity* involves protecting the self-esteem of individuals. *Flexibility* refers to the facilitator's ability to make changes based upon the group's needs or requests. We saw an example of this in the previous section: plan to use the methods listed in the meeting agenda, but be flexible if the group chooses another method. Following is a list of more specific ways to display sensitivity and flexibility, which will both help the group and set an example for how group members should treat each other.

- ▶ **Foster respect for the individual:** "So, from your perspective, Sue, you feel that this guideline is unfair?" Different perspectives are desirable.

- ▶ **Protect individuals from personal attack:** "John, you may disagree with Tim's viewpoint, but let's refrain from personal attacks." Don't allow name-calling or insults to enter the picture.

- ▶ **Encourage a climate of acceptance:** "Based upon June's suggestion, it looks as though the group has yet another idea to consider." Encourage the group to consider new ideas and understand them before judging them.

- ▶ **Observe what the group is doing:** "It looks like we need a break." Watch for a drop in attention, shrugging of the shoulders, frowns, waning interest, tiredness, or participants avoiding eye contact.

- ▶ **Project patience:** "Let's review the time frames we've committed to so we can clear up some of the confusion." Be calm through any difficulties, such as delays or problems.

- ▶ **Adapt to the group's needs:** "Since the group prefers discussing this issue first, that's what we'll do."

- ▶ **Use the group's language:** Always speak and write in terms of the exact wording used by group members.

- ▶ **Reinforce participation:** Don't praise group members for coming up with a good idea, but instead for their involvement: "It's great to see everyone involved—keep it up!"

▶ **Help those with unique needs:** If a group member has an individual or unique need, strive to help out: "Lynn, I know you prefer this in writing, so I'll make arrangements to have this written up for you."

▶ **Make requested changes.** Make changes in the agenda based upon requests or needs. As the facilitator, you make process recommendations, but the group ultimately decides whether it will follow your recommendations.

▶ **View the people in your group as your customers.** This will reinforce how you should treat them as you guide them through the meeting.

There is one group I facilitate that often requires flexibility on my part. A late change in the location or time of our planned session is not unusual. Sometimes, I get there and find the room not yet set up for the meeting or not enough markers for the flip chart. I always arrive early and come prepared with extra markers, flip chart pads, and masking tape. I also make sure I have plenty of patience, because things don't always go perfectly. One reason this group calls me so consistently is because I am flexible and willing to make last-minute changes for them.

> ### Create a Safe Environment
>
> The facilitator creates a safe environment by protecting the self-esteem of all group members.

Displaying Tact

Tact is defined as the ability to deal with people without offending. Sometimes it is necessary to enforce a rule or make suggestions. It is important to do these things in the most positive way possible so as not to alienate anyone. For example, if a group member gets defensive when you remind him or her of a ground rule, then a chance for helping the group function more effectively is lost. Tact can minimize the defensiveness that sometimes materializes when you have to enforce the rules.

Here are a few ways to be tactful:

▶ **Think before you speak.** Consider the possible impact of your words on an individual or the group as you formulate your thoughts.

▶ **Be clear about what you're saying.** Be open and direct—but never hurtful: "We've discussed how interrupting can be destructive. Yet it seems to be something that's difficult to avoid. What can I do to help?"

▶ **Express your observations with humility.** Be careful to qualify them as your opinion, prefacing your comments with a phrase like "It seems to me that …."

▶ **Avoid blurting out what you want to say:** "Hold on! We're going to be here all day at this rate!" Outbursts like this will alienate participants.

Tact Matters

Always maintain self-control by being tactful. If you ever find yourself in an argument with a member of the group, no matter how justified you feel, the others will always side with their colleague.

Here are some of the many situations that call for tact:

▶ When you need to enforce group rules or group commitments: "Bill, remember that we decided not to use acronyms anymore."

▶ To help the group adhere to proper procedures: "Now, group, let's not worry about whether we agree with any of these ideas. We've agreed to list them first, then discuss their value."

▶ To give feedback on the group's behavior: "It seems that there is a lot of sarcasm when dealing with this subject. Why?"

▶ To give direction and guidance to the group: "Could you summarize what you just said in a few words?"

Chapter Summary:
The Group Needs You

This chapter has outlined four key ways to provide a bird's-eye view in order to help group members improve the way they work together and progress toward their stated objective.

Keeping the Participants Aware

The group needs to be kept aware of the stated outcome, time frame, decisions made, progress, group effectiveness, ground rules, and any other pertinent information. You do this by verbalizing and pointing out your observations to the group.

Building Consensus

Consensus is the best type of decision making for group process. The definition of consensus is 100 percent support from all members for a decision made by the group even if all members may not agree 100 percent with that decision.

Maintaining Sensitivity and Flexibility

Sensitivity and flexibility help foster a positive environment. A sensitive and flexible facilitator models respect, protects individuals from personal attack, encourages a climate of acceptance, projects patience, and adapts to the group's needs and language.

Displaying Tact

Facilitators demonstrate tact by thinking before they speak and by expressing their thoughts clearly but with humility. The facilitator must be assertive but tactful when enforcing ground rules, maintaining adherence to procedures, and giving feedback and direction.

The group needs your objectivity and is counting on you to apply a bird's-eye view to the total picture of the meeting. This will allow members to concentrate on voicing their ideas, making decisions, and reaching their desired outcome.

Chapter 5

Let's Agree to Disagree

> "Every time Antonio makes a suggestion, the rest of the team ignores it! How can we complain about his lack of commitment when we never give him an opportunity to really be heard? And we cut people off like this all the time!"

These comments came from a group of engineers I facilitated from a prominent organization in Atlanta. They were experiencing difficulty communicating with each other. Group members often interrupted the people who were introverted. Although there was trouble among group members, the group was able to address this difficulty after one person pointed it out.

Disagreement and conflict can be one of the most frustrating experiences for the group and the facilitator. But it can also be rewarding if handled appropriately and skillfully.

This chapter will explain what conflict is, how groups typically approach conflict, and effective methods for dealing with it. You will learn techniques for creating open discussions around areas of disagreement. As a result, group members will reach solid agreement quickly and decisively.

Conflict is normal and even necessary for a group to work together effectively. Its presence ensures that different options and views are fully explored.

A Case for Conflict

There is a strong business case for conflict. Without it, organizations are arrogant and complacent. Since people are not open to differing ideas, they become inflexible and unable to adapt to change. When faced with competition, revenues can quickly recede, making the organization vulnerable. The presence of conflict means that businesses consider all views before making decisions. When this happens, they are more able to adapt and can survive during economic downturns.

This is critical in making a sound decision. Conflict in and of itself isn't bad; it's how disagreement is handled that can pose a problem.

When there are problems, it's important to get the issues to the surface. Only then can these problems be worked out. The group of engineers I worked with had problems in communicating with each other. Most members felt there was not much listening taking place and quite a bit of talking by everyone at the same time. Resentment started building.

I helped this group by doing two things. First, I suggested that the members discuss their sources of disagreement. They were comfortable doing this openly and honestly. After some in-depth discussion, they concluded that they were not taking enough time to listen to each other. Second, I asked them to identify what could be done to improve in this area. They identified some specific new behaviors that would help them improve their listening. The conflict was resolved constructively and the group became more cohesive and the members worked together more effectively as a result.

What Is Conflict?

There are three types of conflict: process conflict, content conflict, *and* communication-style conflict.

Conflict is a disagreement within the group that is significant enough to slow down or halt the group's progress. There are three types of conflict: *process conflict, content conflict,* and *communication-style conflict.*

Process conflict occurs whenever group members have trouble agreeing on *how* to go about reaching their desired outcome. It can stem from disagreements over things like how often the group should meet or how the group will make decisions.

Content conflict occurs when the group cannot reach a consensus on ideas, alternatives, goals, outcomes, and any business issues that members must agree upon. It can erupt over these actions:

- ▶ Choosing one option from many options
- ▶ Dealing with budget issues
- ▶ Establishing a goal
- ▶ Determining action items needed in an action plan
- ▶ Reaching a consensus on time frames and deadlines
- ▶ Targeting factors that are contributing most to a specific problem

Communication-style conflict occurs when there is a diverse mix of people in the group and a corresponding mix of preferred communication styles. An extroverted person might be perceived by some group members as too talkative, while an introverted person may be perceived as too quiet. Some people like to make decisions quickly and might become frustrated when someone who is analytical takes more time to make a decision. Yet, if most group members are analytical, they may resent being pressed to make a decision by someone who is more decisive. Style differences create much potential for conflict.

While style should not enter into decision making, it is challenging for group members to make decisions on the value of the ideas alone, not on the potentially negative or positive perception of the person presenting them. It is up to the facilitator to recognize this and help members consider all options objectively as they respect each other's differences.

Whenever I work with a group, I look for balance. Group members should complement each other by having a variety of strengths among them. For example, I am a person who can make decisions quickly. This is good because I usually recognize what's important immediately. But I'm not good at consid-

> *While style should not enter into decision making, it is challenging for group members to make decisions on the value of the ideas alone, not on the potentially negative or positive perception of the person presenting them.*

Communication Styles

If you are working with a group on a long-term project, consider using a survey to identify everyone's preferred communication style. The four basic styles are analytical, director, supporter, and influencer. (Several products that help identify communication styles are available for purchase.) By identifying each group member's preferred style, the group will:

1. Have a better understanding of potential conflicts that arise
2. Learn to appreciate differences
3. Utilize the strengths of each person and the group
4. Recognize potential liabilities

ering the details. I tend to make the best decisions when I am working with someone who is more detail-oriented and forces me to slow down to consider all the facts. Groups need this same kind of balance. If all group members think the same way, why would you need a group?

How Groups Respond to Conflict

There are generally three ways in which a group will respond to conflict:

1. Healthy conflict
2. Submerged conflict
3. Chaotic conflict

Healthy conflict is the type of conflict illustrated at the beginning of this chapter. The group members were able to identify their poor listening habits by being open and honest. They then identified what needed to be done to make improvements.

All groups should strive to address conflict in this manner. In this setting, people are comfortable disagreeing with each other. In fact, disagreement is viewed as a necessary and helpful element. While tempers may flare at times, the conflict is almost always resolved and the group is able to progress comfortably. There are no hard feelings because members respect one another's differences. They feel a strong loyalty toward one another and the commitments they have made. Consequently, the group is able to achieve its goals and perform at an extremely high level. The group described at the beginning of this chapter excelled by addressing conflict in this way.

Figure 5-1 illustrates the three responses to conflict. Healthy conflict is in the middle of the spectrum of conflict, with submerged conflict and chaotic conflict on either end.

Submerged conflict occurs when group members are reluctant to bring up controversial issues. A group that submerges conflict can be very challenging for a facilitator to manage. The members never argue, because they are

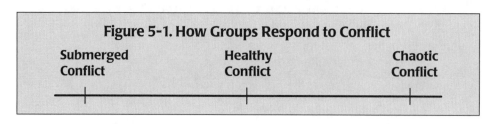

Figure 5-1. How Groups Respond to Conflict

Submerged Conflict	Healthy Conflict	Chaotic Conflict

Group Tendencies

Even if you are working with a group that uses healthy conflict most of the time, it's useful to identify which direction people trend toward. Groups are never perfect, so they have tendencies toward either submerged or chaotic conflict. By being aware of their tendencies, you can help them stay out of trouble.

uncomfortable with conflict. Instead, they tend to reach consensus very quickly, with little discussion. There can be much unspoken resentment and irritation under the surface, however. This plays itself out when group members criticize the group outside the meetings. Group commitment and loyalty are low, progress is slow, and goals often go unattained.

Submerged conflict can be the most challenging situation for the facilitator, because group members refuse to discuss their differences. They prefer to ignore their disagreements, allowing problems to fester and grow. Sadly, the group's true potential is never fully realized. Since people feel that being open is too risky, they convince themselves that the current level of performance is good enough.

Submerged conflict can be the most challenging situation for the facilitator, because group members refuse to discuss their differences.

Be Objective

The facilitator's lack of objectivity can also cause people to shut down and not express disagreement. Members will resent involvement from someone who is expected to be neutral and won't bother to present any opposing ideas.

The members of one group that I worked with were so afraid of being open about their problems that their meetings had many awkward silences. No one wanted to admit that they felt manipulated and intimidated by their manager. Yet, outside of their meetings, they came to me one by one and discussed their issues in private. Since I was the designated facilitator, I was able to listen to each individual's issues and, afterwards, sit down with their manager to discuss what I had learned. Since I did not reveal any names, he was able to focus on the issues along with my recommendations.

Here are some additional ideas for helping a group move from submerged conflict to healthy conflict:

▶ Point out the specific behaviors that characterize submerged conflict and explain why they are not effective: "You seem to have reached this important decision quickly. I'm concerned that there may be some unspoken reservations that will compromise support for this decision." Or "There doesn't seem to be anyone willing to play the devil's advocate when we reach a decision point. Are you sure you're considering all the issues thoroughly?"

▶ Encourage the group to discuss the issues openly and to find areas for disagreement. This will help them make better decisions because they have considered all areas of concern.

▶ If necessary, speak with some of the group members individually to encourage them to be more open.

Groups in which people interact in *chaotic conflict* require help in a different way. Unlike submerged groups, chaotic groups are so comfortable with conflict that members argue excessively. The good news is that a chaotic group is generally open, so you can recognize their chaotic approach. However, they rarely reach a resolution to their disagreement. Group members tend to be loud during their discussions, with a lot of interrupting. Sometimes sarcastic humor runs rampant, and it can inflict pain on the self-esteem of group members. With such an abundance of energy, the group has trouble focusing on its goals.

Arguing for Pleasure

Some people enjoy arguing. They get lost in debate for the sake of debate or the pleasure. Recognize this, because you will have to get them focused back on the issues.

One time a group of creative writers developed the habit of communicating with excessively sarcastic remarks. Some of the group perceived this as a way of displaying the superiority of certain highly regarded members. Their meetings were often loud, with everyone trying to assert their ideas. Once they were able to recognize that sarcasm was rampant and potentially destructive, group members took the next step. They decided not to use sarcasm in their discussions any more. Humor was fine, but whenever sarcasm slipped out, group members comfortably reminded the offender of their mutual commitment to eliminate it. Future interactions were much more positive and, as a result, the group was able to accomplish more.

Chaotic groups are typically very energetic, to the point where they are out of control. They need help harnessing all that energy. Once this is done, they can focus more effectively on achieving their desired objective. Here are some ways you can help:

- ▶ Point out any behavior that is destructive and remind the group members that they must respect one another and all ideas: "There seems to be a lot of sarcasm. How is this impacting you?" Or "I'm noticing quite a lot of interrupting. Has anyone else? What suggestions do you have for improving this?"

- ▶ Praise the group on its high energy level and remind members that they need to focus by listening better and concentrating on the goal: "You have a tremendous amount of energy and enthusiasm. Let's work on focusing that energy by listening to everyone's ideas. We will then be able to achieve our goal more quickly and effectively."

- ▶ Remind the group to eliminate personal attacks and step in to halt any that occur: "One thing we must not tolerate is personal attacks. If you have a concern, please offer it without insult."

Advantages of Chaos

Chaotic groups are easier to facilitate than submerged ones. You always know what's going on in a chaotic group, because the members openly express viewpoints, even if they are out of control. Once they get some structure and begin to focus, there's nothing they can't accomplish.

Interventions

How does the facilitator assist a group in managing conflict? You help a group by making an *intervention*. An intervention is anything the facilitator does or says to alter the behavior of an individual or a group.

When should an intervention be considered? When there is any disagreement, conflict, or concern—whether stated or underlying—consider intervening. You may not always see a clear-cut need for an intervention; consider the following points when deciding whether an intervention should be made.

If there is any disagreement or concern within the group, consider making an intervention. If the issue is a relatively minor one, such as group members arriving late, wait to see if it happens again. There could be a legitimate rea-

An intervention is anything the facilitator does or says to alter the behavior of an individual or a group.

65

son why members were late. However, if tardiness becomes a pattern, make the intervention. Here are examples of situations that might require an intervention:

- ▶ Regular use of sarcasm by the group
- ▶ Constant interrupting by the group
- ▶ Established pattern of tardiness by the group or an individual
- ▶ A regular habit of dominating the discussion by an individual
- ▶ Continued lack of participation by the group or an individual

If any of these examples occurred once, you would not need to make an intervention. Wait to see if a pattern develops. But don't wait too long! Avoiding an intervention when you know one is needed just prolongs the problem and makes it more difficult for the group or individual to make changes when you finally point it out.

When to Intervene

If you're ever in a situation where you aren't sure whether to make an intervention, use this process. Consider the benefits and disadvantages of intervening. Ask yourself, "If I make this intervention, what could happen that would help the group or individual? What could happen that would hurt?" If the benefits outweigh the risks, then make the intervention.

You should *always* make an intervention in two instances.

The first one is if the group's progress toward its desired outcome is stalled. If this occurs, try to analyze what is happening and what's preventing the group from moving forward. For example, if the members have decided to vote to narrow down a list and they can't agree on the number of votes to use, you intervene to break this deadlock. Another example is if the members have to make a decision on whether to follow one course of action or another and can't reach an agreement. You could help by stepping in.

It isn't always easy to figure out what is preventing a group from progressing. If you are noticing a lot of awkward silences, you probably have a group that submerges conflict. If this is delaying the group's progress, you definitely need to check it out. Call a break and mingle with group members with the hope that someone opens up.

An Imperfect Intervention

Making an intervention effectively requires practice and experience! Give yourself permission to make mistakes until you get the process down. But commit yourself to intervening. It's better to make an intervention imperfectly than not make one when the situation calls for it.

There are also times when one or two individuals delay the group's progress. They are probably not aware they have this effect. Someone could be habitually not following one of the ground rules or two group members may be involved in an ongoing conflict. You would need to intervene by speaking with the individuals in private.

The other instance in which you should *always* make an intervention is when there is a personal attack. Whether the group's progress has been delayed or not, a personal attack must be addressed immediately. Point out the negative remark and explain why it is inappropriate, even if it means interrupting the speaker. "We've agreed that personal attacks are not acceptable behavior. Please refrain from the name-calling and stick to the issues."

Situations That Need an Intervention

Once you have analyzed the situation and decided that an intervention is appropriate, identify the objective of your intervention. Interventions apply to three types of situations, each with a different objective: *changing behavior*, *reaching consensus*, and *gaining management support*. Each one requires a slightly different approach.

You intervene to change behavior when one or more group members are doing something that is causing problems or preventing the group from progressing. Examples are being overly dominant during discussions, excessively criticizing the group or each other, communication style conflicts, and repeated interrupting. When an individual is involved, do this intervention in private; when the behavior is widespread, address the intervention to the group as a whole.

The second situation for intervening is when a group has trouble reaching consensus. This occurs when two or more members can't reach agreement on an issue and the progress of the group has been halted. This could result from a disagreement on process or on content issues. In either case, the lack of con-

Interventions apply to three types of situations, each with a different objective: changing behavior, reaching consensus, and gaining management support.

Ground Rules

Ground rules often reinforce the proper behaviors a group needs to be effective. Use them as reinforcement when intervening.

sensus is delaying the group and it can't move forward without resolving their disagreement.

The third situation in which you would intervene is to gain management support. This is done with the group's manager in private. This type of intervention occurs after other interventions have been attempted; you and the group have tried to solve the issue and have not succeeded. This type of intervention must include a suggested plan of action, because managers prefer being presented a problem only if there is also a solution. You know more about the issue than the manager, so it makes sense that you would also have a solution.

Figure 5-2 outlines the three situations that need an intervention. It also gives examples of what to look for in deciding how to intervene. Although a

Figure 5-2. Situations for Interventions

Goal	Who	Behavior
To change behavior	One group member	Never follows a ground rule Constantly interrupts Consistently disagrees Always dominates the conversation Never contributes to the discussion
	Group members	Do not follow a ground rule Constantly interrupt one another Do not contribute to the discussions Have trouble following up with commitments they've made Regularly avoid disagreements
To reach consensus	Two or more members	Cannot reach an agreement on an issue Become angry or frustrated with each other Any problem situation that has not been resolved by the facilitator's repeated interventions
To gain management support		Any problem situation that has not been resolved by the facilitator's repeated interventions

variety of challenges might arise, these three situations give you the most common scenarios.

Intervening to Change Behavior

The more often you facilitate, the more opportunity you will have to make an intervention to change behavior. As you constantly monitor behavior in the group, you will find opportunities to help the members work together more effectively. It is not always comfortable to address what you've observed. Using the process in Figure 5-3 will make it easier.

Figure 5-3. Intervening to Change Behavior

1. Describe your observation. Include positive reinforcement.
2. Get verification and the reason behind what's happening.
3. Ask about the impact of the situation.
4. Ask for ways to improve the situation.

When you intervene with an individual, always do so in private, so you don't put the person on the defensive in front of others. First, describe to the group member what you've observed, while pointing out the positives of the situation. Ask the individual about what is happening and why this behavior is occurring. "There's something I'd like to discuss with you. I've noticed that you are fully engaged in the discussion, but other group members are struggling to participate. Have you noticed this? What do you think is causing this?" You will find that the impact of the person's dominance can be discussed and you can actually get the person's help in promoting more balanced participation: "Your interaction might be used to get others involved. How could we make it easier for others to participate?" If the person has no answer, you could ask him or her to call on the others for input.

When you intervene with an individual, always do so in private, so you don't put the person on the defensive in front of others.

Who's Responsible?

The intervention to change behavior is designed to help the individual become more self-aware. You place responsibility for behavior modification on the individual. Using questions to get commitment for making changes is much more powerful than a directive approach.

I have used this method on a regular basis with individuals. One of my clients was consistently late, did not keep the commitments he made, and was generally making my job difficult. I used this method to point this out, hoping that he would be open to hearing this feedback. He thanked me for being candid and seemed to respect me even more afterwards. We ended up developing a strong working relationship.

> ### Be Careful!
> When making an intervention to change an individual's behavior, you must be more cautious than when you are changing the group's behavior. Use more questions and point out more positives. This prevents hurt feelings and defensiveness.

You can also use this process to point out a widespread pattern of behavior that is slowing the group's productivity. For example, the group of creative writers followed the same steps to address the group as a whole. I guided them through the process.

First, I discussed what I was observing and asked if anyone else noticed the same behavior: "You all have a great sense of humor, but I've noticed some occasional sarcasm in how you communicate. Has anyone else noticed this?" I then gave them time to discuss their observations and what was causing this behavior. After they discussed their perceptions of the issue, I asked, "How do you think this impacts the group as a whole?"

I was ready to point out the impact myself in case group members could not think of anything. However, they quickly realized how destructive their use of sarcasm had been. Some members did not realize they were offending others and felt contrite. I asked them how they could be more effective as a team or what they could do to eliminate this behavior pattern. They concluded that they needed to stop using sarcasm, to add this commitment to their ground rules, and to remind each other if someone forgets.

Intervening to Help Two or More Individuals Reach a Consensus

There will be times when group members will struggle to reach an agreement at a decision point. You can be very valuable in helping them consider the different views and then find an avenue that everyone can support. The following process is a method that can be used to help two or more individuals resolve conflict. *Resolving conflict* means reaching an agreement on how the parties involved will either prevent the conflict from recurring or develop a plan of action to deal with this conflict that is acceptable to all members.

First, get group members to discuss the issue openly and honestly by asking for people to share their views. You could say, "It seems that you are not seeing eye to eye on this issue. Let's discuss why each of you feels the way you do." This will help the group clear up any misunderstandings and clarify both areas of agreement and disagreement. They may need your help in pointing out the specific areas in which they agree and the specific areas in which they disagree. As an example, "It seems that everyone agrees on the date of the product rollout, but many of you are not in agreement on how much to spend on advertising. Am I correct?"

Do We Really Disagree?

When you really listen to two opposing viewpoints, you'll find that there is more agreement than disagreement. Often the two parties don't realize they simply misunderstand what is being argued. It's critical that you apply effective listening skills so that you can:
1. Point out areas of agreement and disagreement
2. Paraphrase what is being said, to generate common understanding
3. Find out whether there is a misunderstanding and clear it up

Getting people to express and analyze each other's views is important. If members at least feel they have been heard and understood, they will be more likely to support a decision that was not their first choice. It may also help people to understand the reason behind each opinion being expressed. This may help the group consider something important that hasn't been mentioned yet.

Once the problem or issue has been thoroughly discussed, get the group to generate possible ideas for resolving the issue. To accomplish this, you might ask one or more of the following questions, depending on the specific issue:

▶ What should you do to make sure this doesn't happen again?

▶ What would have to happen for all of you to support this?

▶ What ideas do you have to prevent this in the future?

If members at least feel they have been heard and understood, they will be more likely to support a decision that was not their first choice.

Figure 5-4. Intervening to Reach Group Consensus
1. Facilitate an open discussion.
2. Verify areas of agreement and disagreement.
3. Ask for ways to resolve the issue.

Once the group has discussed a sufficient number of options for resolving the issue, lead the group to a resolution. The group will hopefully reach a consensus.

Here's a simple example of how the intervention process works. Suppose that group members want to buy a chocolate bar to divide up among themselves, but they don't agree on the kind of chocolate. Subgroup A wants a plain bar and subgroup B wants one with peanuts. As they discuss and clarify all issues, they make a discovery. Subgroup A members don't want a peanut chocolate bar, because they hate peanuts, and subgroup B members don't necessarily have to have a bar with peanuts; any type of nut will do. So the group decides on an almond chocolate bar.

While this is a very simple example, it is not unlike many situations in which groups can't reach a consensus. The facilitator can help a group explore the areas of disagreement fully enough to also realize the areas of agreement. This makes reaching consensus more possible.

For example, imagine a session in which a group of mid-level managers represents two functions in the organization, marketing and engineering. The marketing people are selling services that the engineering department cannot deliver on time. This conflict concerning delivery dates has to be resolved in order to meet customer requirements. A good facilitator can help by generating discussion around marketing's preferred time frames for the specific products. The facilitator would ask the group to generate ideas for how engineering could meet the time frames or how marketing could revise the dates without alienating any customers. After formulating a plan for addressing the problem with delivery times, they might reach an agreement on how they could work more effectively in the future. Marketing would be given specific time frames for specific products (with some negotiating so they can keep up with competition)

True Disagreement

When there is true disagreement, something under the surface is usually contributing to it. People don't typically volunteer these underlying needs, yet they may be driving the disagreement. Ask some probing questions to uncover these personal needs, such as these:

▶ Why is this so important to you?
▶ What's really bothering you?
▶ What will it take to make you more comfortable with this?
▶ What's the most important issue for you?

and engineering would be promised more advance notice on future client requirements. This is a fictitious example, but it shows how a consensus could be reached with a facilitator generating a discussion around the issues.

Intervening to Gain Managerial Support

The intervention that is designed to get management support is used as a last resort. It is needed when you have already intervened to change behavior several times on a specific issue, the behavior remains unchanged, and the group's progress has been seriously delayed. Another instance in which you would need management support is when you have repeatedly intervened to help the group reach a consensus on a specific decision point and group members are still struggling, thus impacting their ability to reach an agreement that everyone can support.

The intervention that is designed to get management support is used as a last resort.

In other words, you use an intervention with the group's manager when you have intervened several times with no success. Here are some examples:

▶ A difficult group member prevents the group from progressing because of his or her behavior. You've already spoken privately with this person on several occasions. He or she has not made any changes for the better.

▶ Difficulties have arisen because group members tend to interrupt each other. You've initiated discussions about this several times. The members just can't seem to make improvements, which has greatly reduced their productivity.

▶ There is an unclear understanding of what management expects the group to accomplish. The group has become paralyzed and is not progressing. You've clarified their areas of confusion, but realize that only their manager can answer these questions for them.

▶ The group needs an unanticipated resource. They need approval from their manager because they don't have the authority to get this resource themselves.

Since managers generally like problems and solutions presented together, Figure 5-5 illustrates the best way to gain managerial support. First, point out the positive aspects of what the group is working on: "We are working within the budget that you've set for us and are considering some cost-saving measures." This will demonstrate the value of the group's contribution. You want the manager to know the group is accomplishing something beneficial.

Figure 5-5. Intervening to Gain Managerial Support

1. Point out the positive aspects and benefits of the group's work.
2. Identify the problem or need.
3. Make your recommendation to address the problem or need.
4. Ask for management approval.

Problem or Excuse?

What's the difference between a complainer and a problem solver? Complainers point out problems and use them as excuses. Problem solvers identify problems and solutions for solving them. Senior managers quickly notice who is in which category and usually reward the latter.

Next, discuss the problem or need clearly and concisely: "We are having a problem with one group member. John Smith's dominating behavior is continuing to be a problem, even though we've discussed this with him at length." Explain the problem and also describe what has already been attempted to resolve the problem.

Then, make your recommendation or suggest a solution and clearly state the anticipated benefit: "I think he should be removed from the group and sent back to his previous job position. This way, the group will be able to finish the project on time." The manager may want to get some additional information from you. Answer his or her questions concisely. Lastly, ask for approval: "Can I get your approval on this?"

I worked with a group of people from a variety of job positions, including both front-line and corporate. One of the corporate people (we'll call him "Joe") was designated as the group's subject-matter expert because of his vast experience. However, Joe was not considered competent in the particular area

---

Answer First

Whenever you have to answer a question (especially from a senior manager), make a point of giving the specific answer *first* and then providing additional support afterwards. If, for example, a senior manager wants to know when the group will be meeting next, give the specific date and time. You can always follow up with additional information, such as what the meeting will focus on. However, you will sound more direct and confident by answering the question first.

---

in which the group needed information. This came up in several discussions when the group needed more expertise from the area he was representing.

After facilitating a very candid discussion in which the group members expressed their concerns without offending Joe, everyone (including Joe) decided that he was not a good match for the group's needs. I went to the manager and recommended that Joe be placed in a different role for the project— one that fit better with his knowledge. I also recommended placing a new member in the group to fulfill the need for a subject-matter expert. Everyone ended up very satisfied with this change, including Joe. He certainly wasn't incompetent; he was simply in the wrong role.

Chapter Summary: Making Conflict Healthy

This chapter has outlined the major types of conflict and the ways in which groups typically address such disagreements. It is important to get group members to verbalize their disagreements in order to resolve them. Conflict is healthy, as long as it is addressed and resolved.

What Is Conflict?

Conflict is a disagreement within the group that is significant enough to slow down or halt the group's progress. The three types of conflict that groups display are process, content, and communication style.

How Groups Respond to Conflict

Groups typically approach conflict by avoiding it (submerged), addressing it (healthy), or excessively arguing about it (chaotic). The facilitator strives to guide the group into the healthy range, where conflict is addressed and resolved.

Interventions

An intervention is anything a facilitator says or does to alter the behavior of an individual or a group. When the problem is relatively minor, the decision to intervene is a judgment call. Making an intervention becomes an obligation when the group's progress is delayed or stalled or when one group member has made a personal attack on another.

Situations That Need an Intervention

There are three situations in which an intervention could be made. The first is to change an established behavior pattern by an individual or a group. The second is to help two or more members reach a consensus when they have had difficulty doing so. The third, an intervention to gain managerial support, is used as a last resort after the first two interventions have failed to produce any improvement.

There is no group whose members will be able to agree on each and every issue that is presented. In order to reach a specified goal, sometimes a group will have to "agree to disagree" and find the solution that has the best chance of gaining support.

Chapter 6

How Can We Get Things Done?

> **D**an, a project manager, ruminates: "All I ever seem to do is put out fires! I keep fixing the same problems over and over again. I can't seem to find time to eliminate the problems. I simply put bandages over them. They inevitably come back to haunt me."

As human beings, we face challenges every day, just like this project manager. Yet, some people seem to overcome obstacles better than others. What gives some of us the ability to set a goal, decide what it will take to reach that goal, and then achieve it? Luck is sometimes a factor, but an unreliable one. Is it talent? Talent does help, but there are many talented people who never seem to be able to accomplish anything.

So, what does it take? A well thought-out, structured plan is the best method for achieving worthy goals for both individuals and groups. People need a bit of structure in order to develop and use their creativity and talent and set goals that will improve the organization. These structures are called *process models*. They contain predetermined steps that illustrate the actions necessary to achieve a goal. These models eliminate frustration because they help groups

> Talent is no guarantee for success. It also takes a concrete plan and discipline.

and individuals deal with issues systematically. This chapter will describe one process model that groups can use to organize their work. It is called PROBE.

In this chapter, you will learn how to guide groups through the phases of PROBE. This model will help you organize the group's approach depending on the type of goal the group wants to achieve. If there is something in the organization that is not working properly, such as equipment breaking down, people not performing their jobs quickly enough, or errors being made, you can guide the group through the PROBE process model to solve the problem. You can also use PROBE to make decisions or take advantage of an opportunity within the organization, such as a new product, designing a new procedure or planning an event. PROBE can be used for either solving problems or addressing opportunities.

Overview of PROBE

Each letter of the PROBE process model represents a specific function. Figure 6-1 shows the letters and phases.

Figure 6-1. The PROBE Process Model

Phases
P—Projection
R—Root Cause Analysis
O—Options
B—Best Options
E—Execution

P stands for *Projection*. It's the first thing that must be done to solve a problem or address an opportunity. You describe the situation and *project* what action will be taken. This is usually done with a measurement, such as reducing errors by 50 percent or increasing product sales by 20 percent.

The next step, *R*, stands for *Root Cause Analysis*, which means finding the real cause of the problem. During this phase, if the group is solving a problem, members collect information to identify factors that may be causing the problem. If the group is addressing an opportunity, there is no need for root cause analysis, so the group skips over this phase and moves on to the next one.

The next phase is *O* or *Options* phase. This is where the group members discuss ideas for eliminating root causes if they are solving a problem or they identify options for address-

> ## Process Models
>
> There are many other process models. The most logical ones contain steps or phases that parallel each other.

ing an opportunity. Once they have identified those options, they evaluate and choose the *Best Options*, which is the *B* phase in the process model.

After group members have evaluated and selected best options, they develop a plan for implementing them. This is the last phase, *E* for *Execution*.

The phases of the PROBE model can be used in a number of ways, depending upon how much authority the group is given or what it is being asked to accomplish.

For example, imagine that senior management asked the group only to identify what is causing unusually low productivity by service technicians. The group would need to use only the first two phases of the PROBE model. As their facilitator, help them develop a projection to define the problem and project exactly how much they think they can increase productivity. It might be helpful to know current productivity levels and compare these with the expected levels. This is the first phase, Projection. Next, you would guide them through the Root Cause Analysis phase to find the source of the problem. At this point they would have fulfilled the management directive.

Another example is if the root cause of the low productivity has already been identified. Imagine that a new piece of equipment used by service technicians is doubling their installation time because they were using it incorrectly. The group is being asked to eliminate the main cause (new equipment being used incorrectly) that is contributing to the problem (low productivity during installations). Since they know the cause, they now have to identify options for eliminating it. This is what takes place in the Options and Best Options phases. You would facilitate as group members identify possible options for eliminating the cause, such as these:

- ▶ Training service technicians on the new equipment
- ▶ Coaching them on the job
- ▶ Sending the new equipment back to the supplier
- ▶ Using the old equipment again

This is the Options phase. In the Best Options phase, group members would decide which of the above solutions is or are the best to implement.

The phases of the PROBE model can be used in a number of ways, depending upon how much authority the group is given or what it is being asked to accomplish.

79

What if a sales group is asked to penetrate a new market? It could use the Options, Best Options, and Execution phases to identify possible markets for penetration, to choose the best markets, and to develop a plan for making it happen.

A final example for using PROBE would be if a decision has been made and the group is simply asked to design a plan for carrying it out. Imagine that your group is asked to have a conference to kick off the unveiling of a new product. This is the Execution phase. You would guide the group toward developing a plan of action for this event.

Of course, the group could be charged with identifying the cause of a problem, deciding how it will be solved, and creating an action plan to solve it. In this case, they would follow the entire PROBE model.

Whether the group is using the entire PROBE process or pieces of it, anticipate that it will need a considerable amount of time.

Whether the group is using the entire PROBE process or pieces of it, anticipate that it will need a considerable amount of time. It could take anywhere from one meeting to 20 meetings or even more, depending upon how much of PROBE it is using and the specific situation. Group members need to work both inside and outside of meetings. For example, if gathering information to find a root cause (R phase), they would decide on what information merits gathering *during* a meeting and then make arrangements to gather it *outside* of a meeting.

Using PROBE Individually

You can also use PROBE as an individual. I use this process model all the time.

After writing the manuscript for this book's first edition, I needed to find a publisher. I followed the Options, Best Options, and Execution steps to help me do this. First, I listed about 200 publishers; this was the Options phase. Next, I chose 60 publishers that might be interested in my manuscript, by looking at the types of books that they typically accepted; this was the Best Options phase. In the Execution phase, I listed all the actions needed to interest these 60 publishers in my work. I put together a package that included a book outline, a cover letter, and the first three chapters of my manuscript. I sent this package out to all 60 publishers, resulting in several offers. All I had left to do was make the final selection.

How to Use PROBE

You will need to fully understand how to use PROBE in order to successfully lead a group in solving problems. You will also want to educate the group members on how it works, so they understand the logic behind it. Understanding when to use the different phases will help you determine where to start. This is the first step in guiding the group toward achieving its goal.

The next step is to select the appropriate process tools. As discussed previously, a process tool is a structured method the group follows when identifying causes of problems, options, and plans for implementing decisions. A common process tool, brainstorming, has been mentioned in this book several times. Figure 6-2 illustrates a repertoire of process tools in each phase of PROBE. The next section describes how each of the process tools is used and under what circumstances to recommend them to the group.

Figure 6-2. PROBE Model Process Tools

1. Develop **P**rojection	Goal statement
2. Find **R**oot Cause	Check sheet, flow chart, or survey
3. List **O**ptions	Brainstorm or round-robin Clarify Combine Categorize
4. Pick **B**est Options	Eliminate the obvious Multi-vote Compare against criteria
5. **E**xecute	Action-plan time line

Develop a Projection

This first phase, Projection, helps group members anticipate what action will be taken (in measurable terms). They would also need to include any limits they must work within and describe how the organization would benefit. This is called a *goal statement*.

Here's an example. I worked with a cable company that was having problems with excessive outages. (Outages occur when an entire geographic area loses the connection going into customer homes.) Company management formed a group to include employees in various job positions who had different perspectives on the problem, including service technicians, customer service reps, a dispatcher, a customer service supervisor, and a service tech supervisor. The group's task was to reach an agreement on what action would be taken, how much of the problem could realistically be solved, what the parameters were, and how the company would benefit from their efforts.

With some input from the operations manager, the group members agreed that they should be able to reduce outages by 25 percent. The operations manager also restricted them with one parameter: they would have to continue their current responsibilities while working to solve this problem and they could not hire or reassign other employees to cover their responsibilities. As their facilitator, I helped them write a goal statement. First, I coached them on how to develop one and then facilitated a discussion in which they decided what the statement would say. Here's what they came up with.

We will reduce outages by 25 percent in a way that maintains current headcount so that our customers will be more satisfied with our service.

How do you help a group write a goal statement like the one that was developed by the cable company group? First, explain to the group that it must include three elements. The group must identify a measurable action that will be taken. They should also explain any parameters that the group must maintain, such as budget, time, productivity, policies, regulations, or headcount. The third element necessary is a description of how the organization will benefit.

It often helps to suggest a structure for the goal statement.

▶ We will ... (Describe the measurable action to be taken.)

The Goal Statement

As you write your goal statement, you may find that you don't need to follow the above structure precisely. As long as you include three elements—a measurable action, parameters, and benefits for the organization—you can phrase the statement without including *we will*, *in a way that*, and *so that*.

- ▶ In a way that ... (Describe any parameters that must be maintained.)
- ▶ So that ... (Describe how the organization will benefit.)

Examples of a Goal Statement

Here are examples of fictitious situations. For each situation there's a correctly written goal statement.

A group from a power company is trying to reduce by 10 percent the number of power outages that occur each quarter. It is working with a tight budget.

Goal statement: We will reduce quarterly outages by 10 percent in a way that maintains our current budget so that we can improve customer satisfaction.

A group from a lumber company is trying to reduce the time it takes to process an order, from three weeks to two weeks. There have been complaints from customers that it takes too long to receive products.

Goal statement: We *will* reduce the product order process by one week *in a way that* maintains current headcount *so that* we can get orders to our customers faster and maintain our current customer base while adding new customers.

A hospital emergency unit has low employee morale. There have been an unusually high number of anonymous employee complaints sent to human resources. Group members want to reduce the complaints by 50 percent. Work on this project must be done during non-peak hours.

Goal statement: We *will* reduce employee complaints by 50 percent *in a way that* these efforts take place during non-peak hours *so that* we can improve employee morale without sacrificing productivity.

A group from a software company is asked to create some new applications for a popular software product. They must create these applications for use by current markets. This will help them create more revenue within current markets.

Goal statement: We *will* identify five new applications for the LINK system *in a way that* will accommodate current markets *so that* the company will have additional revenue streams from current customers.

Meeting Outcome vs. Goal Statement

What is the difference between an intended meeting outcome and a goal statement? A goal statement defines and sets measurable actions for the overall situation. The steps toward achieving these actions (the PROBE model) will be taken during several meetings over a period of time. The intended outcome statements in each of these meetings will point out which step in PROBE the group is currently following during that meeting as it makes its way toward solving the problem.

Achieving the intended meeting outcome versus achieving the overall goal is much like winning the battle versus winning the war. If you win enough battles, you'll probably win the war. Meeting outcome statements are like the small battles you fight in order to reach the overall goal—winning the war. If you achieve enough meeting outcome statements, you'll most likely achieve the overall goal.

Target the Root Cause of the Problem

When you target the root cause, you are trying to find out what is causing a problem.

When you target the root cause, you are trying to find out what is causing a problem. This is something people do in a variety of situations as individuals and as groups.

I like to snow ski—and I'm just good enough to be dangerous. Sometimes, I pick up speed more quickly than I can handle. When I make my turns, I know I'm supposed to dig into the snow with the edges of my skis, but it doesn't always happen.

If I'm having a particularly difficult time doing this, which means I'm making a lot of "face plants" in the snow, I do a quick root cause analysis. First, I check out my boots, because if they're not snug enough, it's more difficult to turn. Then, I make sure I'm leaning into the fronts of my skis enough; this helps with balance. Finally, I evaluate whether I'm digging the edges of my skis into the snow; this gives me control. Usually it's the edges that are the problem. Once I identify what's causing me to lose control over my speed, I can correct the problem. Skiing on my feet is much more fun than skiing on any other body part.

To do root cause analysis well in a business situation, a group must gather and discuss information about the problem, much like I mentally discuss my skiing problem. The group needs to determine the *origin* of the problem, which is defined as the factor or factors contributing the most to the problem. These are considered the root causes. The group must find and eliminate them in order to solve the problem.

Remember: if your group is addressing an opportunity rather than dealing with a problem, then searching for a cause is not necessary. In this case, guide the group past this phase and into the next one—O for Options.

There are many ways to gather information about a problem. We will focus on three process tools used for this purpose: the check sheet, the flow-chart, and the survey.

A *check sheet* is a tool used to keep track of the number of times potential causes of a problem are occurring. Examples of causes that might be monitored are time units, types of defects, or events. Since there is rarely only one cause for a problem, the check sheet will identify how often several potential causes are occurring so that those occurring the most will stand out.

One Exception

There is one time when doing some analysis with an opportunity is required. When a situation calls for market research, a group could use the tools discussed in this section.

When using the check sheet, it's important to both gather data *and* organize the types of data to make analyzing it easier. To help a group develop a check sheet, ask them to identify possible causes that contribute to the problem. As each potential cause surfaces, write it down on the flip chart.

Once the group has reviewed the list of causes and agrees that these are the right causes to investigate, get group members to determine the period of time for which the causes will be tracked: one week, one month, or some other time period. The developed check sheet is then given to those on the job who have the most exposure to what needs to be monitored. Another option would be to get volunteers from the group to go through the records to investigate incidences of the listed causes.

Imagine that the power company that wanted to reduce outages by 10 percent developed a check sheet. This was done during a meeting in which the intended outcome was a check sheet for reducing outages.

Group members brainstormed a list of potential causes for outages. They then gave the list to three group members to begin tracking any outages that had occurred during the previous quarter. Wherever the records showed that

When using the check sheet, it's important to both gather data and organize the types of data to make analyzing it easier.

85

one had occurred, they could research work orders to find out what caused it. They documented these occurrences.

The group met again within two weeks to examine a summary report. Figure 6-3 shows the final numbers that were presented to the group. (This list is only an example and would in actuality be much longer.) Also, after examining the results of the first collection of data, the group might decide to gather some additional data. For example, they may decide to find out which equipment is failing and causing outages, since the number of outages caused by equipment failure was 30. Or they may decide to find out which technician's errors had caused outages, since the check sheet indicates there might be a problem with a technician. You sometimes need several phases of data collection to find the real cause of a problem.

Figure 6-3. Example of a Check Sheet	
Causes of Outages, Third Quarter	Number of Occurrences
Inclement weather	10
Technician's error	15
Traffic accident	8
Equipment breakdown	30
Other	7

The second process tool that could be used in determining root cause is the *flowchart*. It depicts a concept in the format of a picture or diagram and is particularly useful for illustrating procedures or multi-step processes. It presents information about a problem involving work procedures such as a service order process, a billing process, contract administration, the hiring procedure, a payroll process, or even an employee disciplinary process.

If you determine that your group's problem involves how well or how quickly things are carried out in a specific work procedure, then recommend that the group develop a flowchart. Guide the group toward identifying all the steps in the process that require examination in chronological order. Write these steps on the flip chart as group members call them out. Emphasize that they will first identify how things are currently being done, not how they think things should be done. Next, have the group identify the type of function that

Importance of a Good Process

A poorly run process almost always has a negative impact on employee performance. It's virtually impossible for even the best associates to do their jobs effectively when they are using an ineffective work procedure. Once process improvement takes place, employee performance and morale go up.

is taking place within each step: decisions, control/inspection, operation, movement, or delay.

For example, consider the case of the lumber company trying to reduce the time it takes to process orders, from three weeks to two weeks. Group members would most likely decide to analyze what currently occurs in the order process to determine if they can speed things up without increasing errors in the orders. They would need to chart the steps in the current order process. Once this is done, the group would determine where improvements could be made.

Figure 6-4 shows a flowchart that represents an order process. A flowchart should designate who is doing what, the department in which the activity takes place, and the amount of time for each activity. The order process illustrated here indicates it takes approximately 15 business days (three weeks) from the day the order is received to the day the order is shipped. (Figure 6-5 defines the meaning of the symbols used in the flowchart. These symbols indicate the type of function that is taking place in each step.)

Once the group can see the whole picture, it is easier to analyze. Ask the group to look for the following possibilities:

A flowchart should designate who is doing what, the department in which the activity takes place, and the amount of time for each activity.

▶ Are there any steps that are unnecessary and should be eliminated?

▶ Are there any steps that could be combined into one step?

▶ Are there any delays that occur between steps? (Often, the problems lie between the steps, not within them. Encourage the group to examine this.)

▶ Are there steps that occur in the same department within different areas of the process? (If the process begins in accounting and then goes to the warehouse and then back to accounting, it could be possible to keep the process in accounting for all the steps and then send it to the warehouse. This would save time.)

▶ What would the ideal process look like? Sometimes it helps to throw out the current process and start over.

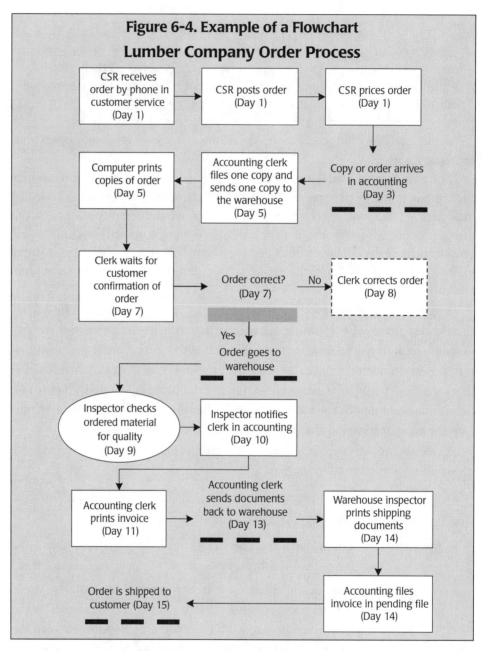

Figure 6-4. Example of a Flowchart
Lumber Company Order Process

After group members have determined ways to improve the process, they can incorporate these changes into the work environment. However, the effect of new procedures should be closely monitored.

The third process tool that helps a group find the root cause is the *survey*.

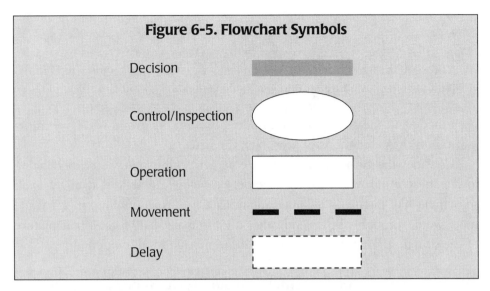

Figure 6-5. Flowchart Symbols

Decision

Control/Inspection

Operation

Movement

Delay

A survey is a list of questions asking people for their opinions on an issue. You would use a survey when there is a negative opinion about some issue and you want to find out what is causing it. It is a common practice for organizations to find out how they can improve the level of service provided to customers by using surveys that ask customers questions about their experiences when doing business with the company. Written surveys can be administered to an entire population or a sample population. Surveys can also be administered by phone, in focus groups, or face to face.

If you are working with a group that wants to find out the perceptions of a specific audience, here's how to do it. First ask the group to identify the questions that should be asked. Write these down and get agreement from the group on both wording and content. After group members have developed their list of questions, ask them who should be surveyed—the entire population or just a sampling? They also need to decide how the survey will be administered: in writing, in person, in focus groups, or over the phone. The group should then decide who will administer the survey, when it will take place, and who will report the results to the group. Once these decisions have

Be Wise

Most organizations must use resources wisely. This means limiting areas for improvement and zeroing in on those few improvements that will have the biggest impact. Avoid working on too many improvement efforts at any one time.

> ## Getting Help
> Market research firms have the expertise to help when you need to use an external source for designing and administering surveys. How would you benefit from using them? Their experience and neutrality ensure valid results.

been made and the survey has been administered, the group will have information on the perceptions of a problem or issue.

Consider the case of the hospital emergency unit that was experiencing low employee morale. If group members developed a survey, it might look something like Figure 6-6. These questions are just a sampling. In actuality, there would probably be several other questions needed to get a true picture of the situation. This survey would be administered to all unit employees.

> ## Figure 6-6. Employee Survey Questions
> Please answer the questions below according to the following scale: 5 is very favorable, 4 is favorable, 3 is average, 2 is low, and 1 is very low.
> 1. How do you rate your company as a place to work?
> 2. How satisfied are you with your job?
> 3. How would you judge the competency of your manager?
> 4. To what extent do you feel you are kept informed of company events?

Whether you and your group use a check sheet, a flowchart, a survey, or some combination of these process tools, once you have identified the root cause or causes, you are ready to move to the next phase of PROBE—identifying options that eliminate these root causes.

List the Options

The Options phase helps groups identify options by eliminating the root causes identified in the Root Cause Analysis phase or address opportunities identified in the Projection phase. The Options phase contains five process tools:

1. Brainstorm to identify possible options
2. Round-robin to identify possible options.
3. Clarify any options that group members don't understand.
4. Combine similar options into one.
5. Categorize if the group needs to organize options into main headings.

Often groups like to evaluate during this phase, which is not a good idea if you want them to fully consider all options available. Remind them that evaluation will take place in the next phase—Best Options. At this point, encourage the group to simply create a list of options and then organize those ideas. There are two process tools that can be used to do this, brainstorming and round-robin.

Creativity

Creativity is very important in the Options phase. Being creative is often a challenging proposition for adults. Yet, young children are naturally creative. If you have spent any time around children, you know what I mean. I love watching my daughter, Mary Beth, when she is painting a picture or sculpting with clay. Children are naturally inquisitive and open to new ideas. Unfortunately, formal education often programs children to produce "the right answers" to receive passing grades. As adults, this focus on "the right answer" can become dominant. We assume out of habit that there is only one right answer to any question. This assumption inhibits creativity and limits you to a narrow field of options. In reality, there are no clear-cut answers.

Brainstorming is defined as a spontaneous generation of ideas from all group members. They say the first thing that comes to their minds and you write down their ideas on the flip chart. Brainstorming is a method that helps group members think of creative ideas with very little structure.

Brainstorming is a method that helps group members think of creative ideas with very little structure.

Make It More Creative!

Brainstorming is naturally a creative process. But you can make it *more* creative by setting some ground rules, such as these:
- ▶ Say the first thing you think of.
- ▶ No idea is ridiculous.
- ▶ Be open to all ideas.
- ▶ Use current ideas to think of additional ones.

If you have a quiet group, try the *round-robin* process tool instead of brainstorming. It gives the group more structure by allowing each group member to give an idea in turn. Just keep going from one group member to the next, one after the other, writing their ideas on the flip chart. If it is Joseph's turn and he doesn't have any ideas, then he can pass. If Benny has an idea, but it isn't his turn yet, encourage him to write it down, so he remembers it. This method makes it easier for silent members to give their ideas and equalizes group participation. Round-robin does not have the same energy level as brainstorming but still encourages group members to give all their ideas, even if they seem like bad ones. Often a bad idea from one person will trigger a good idea from another. Contributing ideas freely enhances creativity.

Round-robin does not have the same energy level as brainstorming but still encourages group members to give all their ideas, even if they seem like bad ones.

Let the Bears Do It

There is a legend being passed around that illustrates the power of the Options phase. A power company was having problems with outages due to ice forming on the lines. A group got together to brainstorm some ideas for solving the problem. A lineman, who had encountered bears while out scaling poles, suggested that they "let the bears do it." They reasoned that if they could get the bears to climb the poles, the climbing would shake the poles and lines, causing the ice to drop to the ground. This one idea triggered more ideas. It was suggested that helicopters could fly over and place a honey pot on top of each pole. This would attract bears and entice them to climb the poles. One member, who had experience with the downdraft from helicopters, suggested flying helicopters over all their power lines, to create wind, which would have the same effect as the bears climbing the poles. What began as a crazy idea turned into a brilliant solution to the problem!

Here's one way to help a group build a list of options. Let's say an independent supermarket is having a problem with wet floors in the refrigeration area. These floors are causing accidents; employees are slipping and falling down. The group created to address the issue knows that the cause is the wet floors. Now it must identify some options for addressing this situation.

Start by asking group members to brainstorm a list of options for eliminating the wet floors in the refrigeration area. As they throw out the ideas, you write them down on the flip chart.

Figure 6-7 illustrates what the initial list might look like.

There are a couple of crazy ideas on this list, but this is a good sign. It means that group members have given their ideas freely and openly. Evaluating the ideas doesn't happen until the next step. You may have to remind group members of this if they start to say things like "That won't work." Also, it's a good idea to number the ideas when writing them down. It makes it easier as participants begin asking you to make changes to the list.

> ### Figure 6-7. Possible Options
> ### to Eliminate the Wet Floors
>
> 1. Maintain refrigeration more frequently
> 2. Mop floors frequently
> 3. Buy newer refrigerators
> 4. Mop equipment frequently
> 5. Place equipment in a low- or no-traffic area
> 6. Put up signs to warn employees
> 7. Put a fence around the area
> 8. Wear flippers
> 9. Put down absorbent rugs
> 10. Don't worry about it

They can reference the ideas by number, so you can find them quickly.

Once the participants start to run out of ideas, it's time to guide them toward *clarifying*, which means making sure all of them understand the ideas that were contributed. Ask, "Which of these items do you need clarification on?" Give them several seconds to look over the list. If a group member asks for clarification of a particular item, refer the question to the contributor: "Who gave this idea? Jerry, could you please explain to Frank what you meant by this?" As Jerry clarifies the idea, write down a brief explanation next to the item being discussed.

> ### Crazy Ideas
> Effective brainstorming often yields some far-fetched ideas. That is actually a *good* sign. It means group members are contributing and accepting all ideas without judging them to be good or bad.

For example, consider the supermarket that had wet floors in the refrigeration area. One group member may ask for clarification of idea No. 4, "Mop equipment frequently." If so, you would need to find out who contributed this idea and then ask that person to explain it to the others.

Participants will still tend to evaluate ideas during clarification. Remind them that they don't have to worry about whether they agree or disagree with any of these ideas until they get to the next phase: Best Options. The clarifying tool is designed to simply help them understand each idea suggested.

> ### Clarification
> You do not have to clarify every single item on a brainstormed list. Clarify only those items that participants don't understand.

After clarifying ideas, the group may need to *combine* some of them. This is necessary when two or more ideas are really the same thing. To find out if they are, ask, "Are there any similar ideas on this list that we could combine as one item?" If there is a suggestion to combine, check with the contributors of the specific ideas before combining them. In Figure 6-7, the group might decide to combine 2 and 4, which both relate to mopping. Then, you would cross out one and leave the other.

It is occasionally necessary for a group to sort ideas into main categories. This is done when the group wants to ensure that the ideas contributed represent specific main headings or themes. First, ask the group to suggest possible categories for the ideas. Then, ask the group to sort the ideas into the suggested categories. Additional ideas or categories may also be generated and added to the list.

For example, the supermarket would categorize the options for eliminating wet floors if group members wanted different employees to have responsibility for the same types of duties. Figure 6-8 shows the different categories assigned to appropriate options. This makes it easier to assign duties, since each employee would be assigned a different category: one person would be in charge of the equipment, another would handle the mopping, and a third would be responsible for putting up the obstacles. The last idea was given a miscellaneous category because it didn't fit into any of the other categories. It will probably end up being eliminated from the list in the next phase, anyway.

> Watch for group members who want to categorize excessively. It's rarely necessary unless the desired objective calls for it.

Figure 6-8. Options in Categories

1. Maintain refrigeration more frequently—Equipment
2. Mop floors frequently—Mopping
3. Buy newer refrigerators—Equipment
4. Mop equipment frequently—Mopping
5. Place equipment in a low- or no-traffic area—Equipment
6. Put up signs to warn employees—Obstacles
7. Put a fence around the area—Obstacles
8. Wear flippers—Obstacles
9. Put down absorbent rugs—Obstacles
10. Don't worry about it—Miscellaneous

Once the group has created an organized list of options, it is ready to evaluate those options and pick the best ones, which is the next phase.

Choose the Best Options

There are three process tools that help a group narrow down a list of options: *eliminate the obvious*, *multi-vote*, and *compare against criteria*. These three tools provide a structure in which the group evaluates the options that were created and organized in the previous phase.

To *eliminate the obvious*, you take a poll to find out which options group members can agree to remove from the list. This is a tool I have used frequently. It's easy to use and helps drop from further consideration items that are obviously not viable. I simply ask the group, "Which items on this list can we all quickly agree to remove because they won't work?"

There are three process tools that help a group narrow down a list of options: eliminate the obvious, *multi-vote*, and compare against criteria.

Look at Figure 6-7. Imagine that, after you ask the group which items can be eliminated, Leo suggests "Wear flippers." Check with the group to make sure there is agreement: "Is everyone in agreement that we can eliminate wearing flippers?" If everyone agrees, draw a line through the item in question. Then ask if anything else can be eliminated. If Lana suggests eliminating another item, "Put down absorbent rugs," you would again check with the others. If anyone has reservations about this new suggestion, you would say, "Let's leave it up there for now."

Eliminating the obvious is used to eliminate only those items that clearly won't work. If there is a reservation from any one member, the item should be left on the list for future consideration.

> **Elimination**
>
> Once you begin narrowing down the list, the elimination tool should be used *first*, before any other tool. It helps the list become shorter and easier to manage.

The next process tool to use is the *multi-vote*. This is a method used to help a group narrow a list and determine the most important options by voting.

Recommend the number of votes each group member can cast. The number should, of course, be less than the number of items on the list. It can be a random number, but a good practice is to divide the number of items by three. So, if there are 10 options on the list, each member could vote for three. You can also allow them to cast up to a certain number of votes on any one option.

In this example, members might be allowed to cast two votes for one option and one vote for another or even all three votes for a single option.

Give participants a few minutes to decide how they will vote. They may want to jot down their choices on scrap paper. Tabulate the votes by calling out each item on the list and asking for a show of hands. Write down next to each option listed on the flip chart the number of votes it receives. This tabulation of votes shows which options are of greatest interest to the group.

Tabulating Votes Properly

Avoid asking each group member one at a time for his or her votes, as this would affect the validity of the voting process. The last few members polled would have an opportunity to change their votes, after seeing the initial results. It's best to tabulate votes item by item, calling out each item on the list and asking for a show of hands.

Figure 6-9 shows the supermarket list with the tabulation of votes. In reviewing this list, you will see that the group clearly wants to handle the problem by focusing on the refrigeration equipment and mopping, because these items received the most votes.

Figure 6-9. List of Options

1. Maintain refrigeration more frequently - 15
2. Mop floors frequently - 10
3. Buy newer refrigerators - 5
4. Mop equipment frequently - 12
5. Place equipment in a low- or no-traffic area - 14
6. Put up signs to warn employees - 4
7. Put a fence around the area - 1
8. Wear flippers - 0
9. Put down absorbent rugs - 0
10. Don't worry about it - 0

Multi-voting can also be used to prioritize a list, ranking items from most important to least important, or vice versa. To do this, follow the process for voting to narrow a list. Once the votes have been tabulated, remind group members they will keep everything on the list, but they have to rank order them. The item with the most votes would be put at the top of the list, the item with the second-most votes would go next, and so on. If any items are tied, the group would decide which one goes before the other. Figure 6-10 shows the supermarket's list of options in a prioritized format.

Figure 6-10. List of Options Prioritized

1. Maintain refrigeration more frequently (15)
2. Place equipment in a low- or no-traffic area (14)
3. Mop equipment frequently (12)
4. Mop floors frequently (10)
5. Buy newer refrigerators (5)
6. Put up signs to warn employees (4)
7. Put a fence around the area (1)

Another tool that can be used to choose the best options is to *compare against criteria*. This process tool helps the group identify criteria against which to compare their options. It works best after the group has eliminated the obvious and multi-voted to narrow the list first. Then, when there are three to eight items left, the group can compare against selected criteria.

First, ask group members to identify some criterion that they think is important in choosing the best options. Write down their ideas on the flip chart. Then introduce a scale from zero to three to measure the extent to which each of the options meets each of the criteria. This gives a picture of how the options compare in terms of the criteria. Figure 6-11 gives an example of how this tool worked with a group of hiring managers who were choosing the best candidates for three account executive positions. It's clear from the "Total" column that the top three candidates are Carol, Vincent, and Lisa.

Comparing against criteria gives groups a way of objectively choosing the best options and it ensures that there is some discussion around them.

Even if the group does not compare against criteria, members should thoroughly discuss the pros and cons of each of the options until they reach a consensus. We have discussed how to help a group reach a consensus in Chapters 4 and 5. Here is a review of some of them:

▶ Ask for input from every participant, so the group can consider all sides of the issue.

▶ When there is a disagreement, ask those with opposing opinions to explain why they have a particular opinion.

Figure 6-11. Compare Against Criteria

	Years in Sales	High Energy	Self-Motivated	MBA	Total
Gina	2	2	2	2	8
Dave	3	1	2	0	6
Lisa	2	3	3	3	11
Carol	3	3	3	3	12
Vincent	3	3	3	3	12

0 = does not meet criterion, 1= partially meets criterion,
2 = meets criterion, 3 = exceeds criterion

▶ Discourage the group from voting at the point when only two or three options are left and the group must choose one. Encourage discussion instead.

Using Tools to Meet Needs

Some people ask whether certain tools can be used in different phases of PROBE. If you are comfortable using this process model and are clear on what has to be accomplished, go ahead. For example, comparing against criteria might be used before the Options phase if you want to limit the ideas under consideration. People will then contribute only ideas that meet certain criteria.

Although it is often difficult for a group to make a decision, members are responsible for their own success. You cannot make the decision for them. You can only strive to help them consider all the issues and support them in whatever decision is made.

Execute the Best Options

One question I am constantly asked is how I started my consulting and training business. In June of 1985, I was single, I lived in a small apartment, and I was out of a job. It was a scary scenario! How I got myself into this situation is of no consequence now, but how I got myself out of it is relevant. I had always had a dream of starting my own consulting business. I figured that it was time to give it my best shot. I set up an office on my dining room table, made some phone calls, and starting asking lots of questions of consultants I knew. From these discussions, I selected my best options and developed a plan of action. I identified everything I needed to do to get my business started, and then I executed my plan. I knew I wasn't the most talented, the most well-known, or the most aggressive consultant. But where there's a will—and an action plan—there's a way! Over the course of the last 19 years, I've been greatly rewarded for following through on that plan and I've had more fun than I ever imagined.

Action planning is what occurs in the Execution phase, once group members have decided on the best options. Now it's time for them to make things happen by implementing their decisions, as I did with my consulting practice. There is basically one process tool for this phase, the *action-plan time line*.

Action planning is what occurs in the Execution phase, once group members have decided on the best options.

An action plan is a logical sequence of activities for implementing a decision and following through on it. An action plan is a schedule that outlines the tasks that need to be done, who is responsible for doing them, and when each of these tasks will be completed. The timing of the activities can be depicted in a graph or on a time line.

To help a group produce an action-plan time line, first clarify the group's decision. Then ask everyone to identify the actions needed to carry it out. Write down their suggestions on the flip chart. Once the participants have agreed with the activities listed, ask them to sequence them so they can be listed chronologically—what needs to be done first, second, third and so on. Next, ask for volunteers to take responsibility for carrying out each of the activities. Finally, ask the volunteers to commit to a completion date.

Figure 6-12 is an example of an action-plan time line. The project shown is a plan to train employees on new equipment. This phase is typically very rewarding, since group members are able to witness the results of their efforts.

Chapter Summary:
Tools for Organizational Improvement

PROBE is a flexible, straightforward process model that groups can use either to solve business problems or to address business opportunities. Business problems occur when something is not working properly, such as excessive errors, low productivity, or excessive complaints due to low customer satisfaction. A business opportunity requires attention because of a potential advan-

Figure 6-12. Action Plan Time Line

Weeks into the Project

Activity	0	1	2	3	4	5	Who
1. Analyze needs	■						Faiola
2. Specify objectives		■					Johnson
3. Choose trainer			■				Popowski
4. Purchase materials			■				Towey
5. Conduct training				■			Tate
6. Assess results					■		Gray

tage that could be created. Examples of business opportunities are developing new product lines, increasing market share, looking for ways to stay ahead of the competition, or planning important events.

How to Use PROBE

To use PROBE, first guide the group into the P step and help them develop a *Projection* for what is to be accomplished. Then, if the group is dealing with a problem, move them to the *Root Cause Analysis* phase to analyze what is creating the problem. (If the group is dealing with an opportunity, skip this phase.) In the *Options* phase, the group creates solutions to reach its goal. The group then moves into the *Best Options* phase to select the most viable solutions. Lastly, in the *Execution* phase the group develops a plan to implement the options selected.

Chapter 7

Meetings and Technology

Roger is an executive editor and works at big publishing company in New York. In order to attract the editorial talent his company needs to prosper, he has allowed several employees to work from their homes around the country. This means that he can't often meet face to face with these people, even though meetings with various groups throughout the organization are important. Fortunately, modern technology is now available to make these meetings possible. Roger just has to learn which technology is most appropriate for what needs to get accomplished between those who work away from the office and people in different functional areas that work at the home office.

There are several technologies that can serve as alternatives to face-to-face meetings. Business professionals use these alternatives regularly because of several factors:

▶ Face-to-face meetings can be expensive, especially when participants must travel to the location.

▶ With more and more people telecommuting (working from a home office), it's often difficult to get participants to the same location, even when everyone is based in the same general vicinity.

▶ There is so little time and so much to accomplish, as organizations constantly face restructuring and downsizing.

With all of these challenges, it is logical to consider easier and more practical options for conducting meetings.

This chapter will outline the various alternatives to a face-to-face meeting, including the advantages and disadvantages of each. You will also get some tips on how to prepare for and conduct meetings through each of these media as well as the situations in which each medium works best.

There are four meeting alternatives; they each use some type of technology to compensate for the lack of face-to-face contact.

There are four meeting alternatives; they each use some type of technology to compensate for the lack of face-to-face contact. The conference call is by far the most commonly used option. The videoconference is also used, but not as frequently. Web conferences are just beginning to become more popular. The medium the least used is called the distributed meeting.

Conference Call

The conference call is a meeting that takes place over the telephone. It can occur with the meeting leader at one site (with any participants at that location) and participants at another site or at multiple sites. It's also common for a face-to-face meeting to include an individual or a group participating by telephone.

Conference calls are becoming more common as organizations become more budget-conscious. The conference call is a practical way to get people together from different locations when a face-to-face meeting isn't possible or practical. Figure 7-1 shows both the advantages and disadvantages of using a conference call. Use it to determine when a conference call is appropriate and when a face-to-face meeting is better.

The technology needed for a conference call is simple, straightforward, and inexpensive. If the participants are at only two locations, it's easy to use a

---

The Future of Conferencing

You can count on having more conference calls in the future. There are several factors contributing to this increase:
  ▶ More people are working out of their homes (telecommuting).
  ▶ Organizations are expanding into new geographical areas.
  ▶ There's greater emphasis on reducing operating expenses.
  ▶ Demands on our time are increasing.

Figure 7-1. Advantages and Disadvantages of Conference Calls	
Advantages	Disadvantages
People who are spread out geographically can be involved.	It's challenging to build relationships.
The meeting can be scheduled to take place immediately.	You can't tell if all participants are engaged.
A smaller group is usually involved.	You can't interpret participants' reactions through their body language.
The cost of a conference call is lower (because there are no travel expenses and conferencing usually takes less time than a face-to-face meeting).	It's difficult when the group is large.
Participants tend to focus strictly on the issues.	It's difficult to ask questions.
Participants don't have to be concerned with how they're dressed.	It's challenging to address volatile or confidential issues.

speakerphone at each. With more than two locations, use a service that gives you a bridge number that participants use to dial in.

There are some specific guidelines to follow for conference calls. During your planning phase, prepare a meeting announcement. Include the dial-in number participants will need to join the conference call. Also attach an agenda and any visuals you plan to use, so your participants will have them for reference during the call. This could include online reference materials with appropriate links.

Do a dry run with the equipment set up to make sure that everything works properly. You may also want to prepare a detailed outline of what you plan to say. You can incorporate these detailed notes into your agenda. Plan to make brief notes to capture what is being said during the call, so you have something for referencing items discussed. Both of these practices will help you come across with confidence.

Another confidence builder is to dial in early and be ready to go, so you can greet the participants as they arrive. You will be better prepared and better received by the participants because you're organized and punctual.

Open your conference call within five minutes of the start time. This will help keep the conference on schedule. As part of your introduction, be sure to do the following:

▶ Conduct a roll call to determine that all invited participants are present.

▶ Make or request brief introductions, if necessary.

If anyone arrives late, offer to catch him or her up later. This way, you won't throw the group off schedule by repeating what has already been discussed. If the conference call is lengthy, schedule short breaks every hour or so.

These guidelines will help you keep the discussion organized.

▶ Identify yourself before beginning to speak, so the participants have a chance to recognize your voice. Encourage all the participants to do the same before they speak.

▶ Pause after asking a question, to allow time for the participants to speak without talking over each other or you. Encourage questions by saying, "I am pausing to see what questions you have up to this point" or "What questions do you have?" You should do this after presenting information for several minutes.

▶ Use mostly open questions when soliciting input. This encourages more than just one-word answers and opens the participants up to sharing more information.

▶ Avoid distracting noises such as shuffling or eating. The microphone is very sensitive and will broadcast noises. Also, cell phones don't work well on conference calls because of all the static that can be transmitted.

▶ Encourage the participants to use the mute button when having side conversations, so as not to distract participants in other locations. But discourage overuse, which allows participants to "tune out."

▶ Remind the participants not to use the hold button if they need to leave the line, because most hold systems play recorded music.

When the discussion during a conference call is orderly and efficient, you will find that you can accomplish more than in a face-to-face meeting.

When the discussion during a conference call is orderly and efficient, you will find that you can accomplish more than in a face-to-face meeting. There isn't

> ## Staying Focused
>
> Sometimes it's impossible to avoid interruptions when conducting a conference call. But the next time you schedule one, post an "In Conference Call" sign on your office. This will prevent people from walking in during your call.

as much temptation to get off track. Participants typically want to attend to the business at hand and then get on to other commitments and responsibilities. For more, see Figure 7-1 on advantages and disadvantages of conference calls.

> ## Length for a Conference Call
>
> The maximum suggested length for a conference call is 90 minutes. If your call goes much longer, you have to call a break. However, it's especially difficult to get participants back on the call after a 10- or 15-minute break.

Videoconference

A videoconference uses technology for voice and video to conduct meetings. Participants are stationed at different locations but can view the facilitator, hear the facilitator, and even view visuals on their monitors. The facilitator can also view participants, which creates a face-to-face dynamic. But the videoconference is still more impersonal than a meeting in person. Videoconferencing is more expensive than a simple conference call, because it requires more technology, which represents additional cost. The actual expense depends upon whether your organization already has the necessary equipment in the conference locations or leases it from a vendor.

Videoconferencing is more expensive than a simple conference call, because it requires more technology, which represents additional cost.

In order to conduct a videoconference effectively, preparation is critical. Remember to send out in advance all the information that the participants will need to connect into the conference. The equipment should also be tested ahead of time and you should familiarize yourself with the conference control panel. Since the participants will see you on their monitors, avoid wearing plaids, prints, stripes, or bright colors. They tend to bleed or create vibration on the screen. Opt for pastel, solid colors. Avoid white, unless you wear a jacket, because it will create a glare.

Once the videoconference begins, you will notice that the participants will be looking at your image on their monitors and not at their cameras. Because of this, they will not be making direct eye contact with you. This may seem strange until you get used to it.

The way you interact on a videoconference is similar to the way you interact on a simple conference call. You must give participants time to respond, since there is a slight delay because the video is not transmitted instantaneously. Since the equipment is voice-activated, it is important to pause occasionally to give participants a chance to respond or ask questions. Identify yourself before you speak and avoid distracting noises that will be picked up by a sensitive microphone.

Visuals can be displayed by a separate camera, but let the participants know when you are displaying them. Make sure your visuals are clear and crisp, with only the most important information. A visual with too much text will look busy and be difficult to see. It's often still best to send out visuals ahead of time, because the video quality is not always good.

Web Conference

Once the equipment has been set up and tested, the Web conference can be run like a conference call.

The Web conference is a medium that uses the Internet or an intranet. All of the participants have access to one site that enables both audio conferencing and video displays. The participants can talk to each other and look at information, but they can't see one another. This is becoming more and more popular, because it combines the impact of visual information and the convenience of a conference call.

Once the equipment has been set up and tested, the Web conference can be run like a conference call. Review the conference call guidelines in this chapter to get some tips.

Distributed Meeting

The distributed meeting, also known as an asynchronous or virtual meeting, provides the most flexible medium for attending a meeting. The participants access an Internet or intranet site from any location at any time. They work from their desktops in small groups or individually. These meetings tend to run over several hours, days, or weeks. The participants move through a series of agenda items that are controlled by the facilitator. They can also view and comment on responses from other participants who have participated up to that point. The facilitator is responsible for managing the technology, structuring the agenda, questions and activities of the participants, and ensuring that all of the members of the group are participating and following the agenda.

Here are some guidelines for organizing and conducting a distributed meeting:

1. Have technical resources available to help manage the technology. There are often problems that arise.
2. Find a good vendor that will allow you to test the equipment and try out some agendas before actually using it for a meeting.
3. Provide examples of the kinds of ideas or responses you are looking for when asking a question.
4. Test your questions on one or two participants ahead of time.
5. Make sure the participants have the necessary background information to participate in the meeting.

The distributed meeting is best used for gathering ideas or getting difficult issues discussed. Since responses are anonymous (unless the participants identify themselves), the participants can evaluate the ideas being presented objectively. Avoid using a distributed meeting when there is a need to build relationships or when talking just makes more sense. You may also find that people resist participating on a network when they would prefer a conference call or some alternative they view as more practical and less time-consuming. A distributed meeting could last for several days before any resolution is reached, but a conference rarely lasts for more than one day.

Avoid using a distributed meeting when there is a need to build relationships or when talking just makes more sense.

Choosing a Meeting Format

Figure 7-2 outlines the main advantages and disadvantages of the four types of meetings discussed in this chapter and the traditional, face-to-face meeting.

Figure 7-2. Advantages and Disadvantages of Different Types of Meetings		
Meeting Type	**Advantages**	**Disadvantages**
Face-to-Face	Easy to discuss sensitive issues Easy to read people Conducive to building relationships	Participants might have to travel to the meeting site Participants do not evaluate ideas objectively
(Continued on next page)		

Meeting Type	Advantages	Disadvantages
Conference Call	Participants can plug into the call from anywhere; no travel is required Tends to be shorter than most other meeting types	Difficult to read people or discuss sensitive issues Difficult to get all participants focused and paying attention
Videoconference	Participants can see each other and visuals Participants can connect from multiple locations	More impersonal than a face-to-face live meeting Equipment is more complicated Cost could be a factor
Web Conference	Participants can connect from their desktops and view information being displayed	More impersonal Can t read participants
Distributed/ Asynchronous Meeting	Participants can participate from anywhere at any time that is convenient	Could take several days for the meeting to end

Figure 7-2. Advantages and Disadvantages of Different Types of Meetings (continued)

Chapter Summary:
Technology for Meetings

There are several alternatives to a face-to-face meeting. The conference call is the most popular, the most practical, and the least expensive. Depending upon the need for the meeting, a videoconference may be the right choice, because you are able to view visuals and people from multiple locations. The Web conference is more like a conference call taking place over the Internet or intranet. Participants can talk to each other and view information on their desktops. The distributed meeting is the most flexible type of meeting. Participants can connect to the meeting from any desktop at any time. The meeting takes place for an extended period of time until everyone has had a chance to input their ideas and comment on other's ideas.

Consider the outcome of your meeting, the desired dynamics, your budget, and what the participants have to do to make the meeting successful. Then you will be able to choose the right medium.

Chapter 8

Should We Form a Team?

Albert: "Hold on a second. There's no way we can be expected to fix this problem. We don't have the budget and we surely don't have the time. Why can't they just hire someone to come in here and fix it? They're not going to agree with our solution, anyway!"

Michael: "I agree. This is a waste of our time!"

If you were the facilitator of this group, you would probably be wishing you were somewhere else. Indeed, several questions must be answered if this team is going to continue working on the project they've been assigned. These two team members need evidence that management will support them by supplying needed resources and backing up any solutions that are developed.

This chapter will address the issue of getting management support and how you can help team members achieve their goals. We will also discuss elements to consider when forming a team, types of teams, and how teams work. If you are involved in forming teams for either permanent or temporary purposes, this chapter explains how to do this effectively. As you read through these guidelines, you may find that the group you work with isn't called a team but exemplifies the characteristics of one. Use whatever information will help you make your group or team more effective.

> ### Team Tennis
>
> As a long-time member of the Atlanta Lawn Tennis Association (ALTA), I have played on a number of teams, even winning the city championships several times. Some of the teams I played on were much more enjoyable than others. When team players practiced together regularly, and supported each other during competitive matches, the team was more cohesive. Groups like this stayed together for years. Sooner or later, most people learn about the importance of creating cohesiveness. Success typically occurs when all individuals are willing to contribute equally and support each other fully.

What is a team? It is a group of people who work interdependently for a common purpose and have been given the authority to solve problems and address opportunities within the organization. Each individual is aware of how his or her contribution fits in with the group's overall objective.

There are many examples of the "team" concept in America. What did it take to get a man on the moon and safely back down again? How do presidential candidates win elections? How is it that some marriages strengthen and survive through years of adversity and challenge? We have all witnessed models of superior teamwork in some aspect of our lives. Most of us have been part of a team experience at one time or another and have benefited from successful teamwork.

Teams in Corporate America

One of the significant changes that has occurred in corporate America in the last 25 years has been the emergence of work teams.

One of the significant changes that has occurred in corporate America in the last 25 years has been the emergence of work teams. Under the influence of such management gurus as W. Edwards Deming, who helped the Japanese rebuild following World War II, and the development of the Malcolm Baldrige National Quality Award in 1987, the emphasis on achieving quality through the use of work teams in business has become common.

More and more American companies are jumping on the bandwagon and implementing the work-team concept to improve their businesses. Look around and you will quickly see the formation of groups for both temporary purposes and long-term objectives. Often, they are not referred to as teams, but named in relation to the function taking place. Regardless of the name, these teams have changed the decision-making hierarchy; corporations are no

---

> ## Enter the Facilitator
>
> A competent, knowledgeable facilitator can make a gigantic difference in a team's effectiveness. Even though the team itself is ultimately responsible for the success of a project, the facilitator can guide people toward cooperation, improve communication between team members and top management, and ensure that everyone supports decisions made. Because facilitators focus on how team members work together, they can educate members on how to work together more effectively.

longer making all the decisions at the top. Decision-making authority is being pushed down to levels closest to the customer to create a greater sense of employee ownership and commitment to the job.

Many companies are forming work teams for the first time, training them inadequately or not at all, assigning facilitators, and telling the teams they're ready to go! Then, when the groups fail, they blame the people involved or the general team concept, and not the real cause: the lack of knowledge and skills needed to develop and manage a successful team.

When utilized properly, a team can accomplish much more than the sum of its individual members.

The Realities of Teams

When utilized properly, a team can accomplish much more than the sum of its individual members. This is called *synergy*: the whole is greater than the sum of its parts. Following is a list of potential problem areas that a team might address or improve:

Increasing Productivity

- ▶ Equipment downtime
- ▶ Maintenance delays
- ▶ Installation problems
- ▶ Shipment delays
- ▶ Customer service delays
- ▶ Slow cycle times
- ▶ Delayed patient care
- ▶ Untimely lab reports

Reducing Errors

- ▶ Reports
- ▶ Billing

- Customer orders
- Supply quality
- Customer service needs

Eliminating Waste

- Unnecessary procedures
- Excessive expenses
- Services not valued by the customer

There is no limit to what a team can accomplish. However, some guidelines should be considered when determining when or if a team is needed:

1. There should be enough time to allow a team to work effectively on an issue.
2. The specific business issue or problem should have more than one possible solution.
3. The project should be too large in scope for any one person to accomplish.
4. Management should be committed to the successful achievement of the goal.

The Power of Groups

Organizations must be able to thrive in competitive markets. Sound decisions on how to do this typically take place when groups of people are collaborating. An individual's decision is rarely as effective as a group's decision.

The consequences of using a team when one is not really needed can be devastating, even if not immediately obvious.

Just as there is an ideal set of circumstances for organizing a team, there are also instances in which the organization of a team would be inappropriate. A work team is not needed:

- Just because using teams is the latest management technique
- When the issue at hand is more suited to the control or expertise of one person
- When you have already decided on a solution to a particular problem and just want group commitment
- When you are facing an urgent situation with a short time frame

The consequences of using a team when one is not really needed can be devastating, even if not immediately obvious. For example, imagine that a customer service manager has selected a new headpiece for his customer service representatives (CSRs) to use. However, he wants to get the new headpiece "blessed" by his CSRs, so he calls a meeting.

At the beginning of the meeting, he tells them that they will decide on whether to purchase the headpiece he is considering. The CSRs don't like his choice and actually prefer another model—one that is more expensive. The manager decides to stay with his original choice.

If this example had actually happened, the CSRs would end up resenting his decision. They would realize that he was going with his original selection, whether they agreed with that choice or not. They would wonder why he bothered to ask them their opinion in the first place. The manager would suffer a loss of credibility and create a situation that would encourage CSRs to continue to complain about the new equipment.

I often hear this complaint. Rather than asking for a team opinion, members reason, a manager should present his or her decision and explain why it is the best option available. In other words, don't ask for input when you don't really want to hear it.

Types of Teams

There are two types of teams: *permanent* and *temporary*. Each is appropriate in different situations, based upon the environment and the nature of the desired objective.

A *permanent team* contains members who work together on an ongoing basis. For example, a team of power plant employees might have the permanent responsibility of monitoring and improving the performance of the plant's equipment.

A *temporary team* contains members who are brought together for a specific purpose or project that has a beginning and an end. When the project is over, the team members go their separate ways. An example of a temporary team is one brought together to create a more user-friendly billing system.

Whether they are permanent or temporary, team members can be *functional*, *cross-functional*, or *multi-functional*.

Functional teams consist of individuals who hold the same job title and possess similar job skills. They often work in the same area, are assigned to one portion of a work procedure, and perform the same tasks. For example, since a payroll procedure can be a complex process in a large company, there are typically several employees assigned to key in weekly wages and generate checks. When brought together as a team, they could be asked to find ways to reduce errors. Another example of a functional team might be a group of cable technicians assigned the task of reducing reworks on service calls.

Cross-functional teams are made up of individuals who are assigned to different departments and have different skills and different jobs, but who contribute to the same work procedure. An example would be a team formed to reduce errors in a billing system. In a typical organization, several people in various departments work on different aspects of the billing system, so it would be appropriate to form a team with members who contribute to different portions of it. Team members might include the telephone service representative who initiates an invoice after a customer calls to place an order or the service representative who fills the order. Another likely team member would be the accounting manager who generates the invoice that is mailed to the customer. Those who could contribute to improved customer service would make qualified team members. Cross-functional teams are effective when a company wants to improve an entire work procedure by increasing productivity, improving quality, or eliminating waste across departments.

Cross-functional teams are effective when a company wants to improve an entire work procedure by increasing productivity, improving quality, or eliminating waste across departments.

A cross-functional team could also be composed of members of the same department who contribute to the same work process, but who perform different tasks and have different responsibilities. Since they do not all have the same knowledge, when one person goes on vacation, that particular person's work does not get done. In this way, cross-functional teams are often at a disadvantage. Because of this, many companies today are striving to train all cross-functional employees to perform all the varied tasks carried out in a particular department. When this occurs, the team becomes multi-functional.

Uncommon Teams

Unfortunately, multi-functional teams are rare in today's work environment. Structural change and time constraints have made it difficult for organizations to train everyone to the same skill level.

Multi-functional teams are made up of team members who individually possess all of the skills required to complete an entire work procedure. One example of this is contract administrators. There is usually a long process used by large companies to develop, initiate, monitor, and enforce contracts with suppliers. Since each team member understands how to perform all of the job functions related to it, individuals work together closely. Employees provide support to one another when needed, even though they each have their own contract assignments. This type of team is very versatile because each member can perform all of the work functions in one entire work procedure. When one team member is on vacation, his or her responsibilities are still carried out, since all team members have the knowledge to perform all positions in their work area.

What do teams actually focus on? The typical corporate environment is made of *internal* and *external suppliers* and *internal* and *external customers*. The typical work team is brought together for purposes of managing the system between the supplier and customer. Figure 8-1 illustrates the relationship among suppliers, teams, and customers.

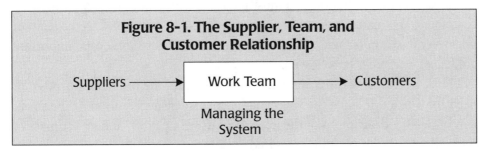

Figure 8-1. The Supplier, Team, and Customer Relationship

Suppliers ⟶ Work Team ⟶ Customers

Managing the System

The term *internal* refers to entities inside the organization while the word *external* refers to those that are outside. A supplier provides the work team goods and services that are needed to perform a function. The team prepares these goods and services for use by the customer. An *internal supplier* might be the warehouse employee who provides technicians with the equipment they need to provide service to their customers. In this example, the equipment provided by the warehouse staff must be in good working order, must be delivered on time, and must meet the exact specifications required by the technicians.

An *external supplier* might be a contract employee who doesn't work for the organization, but is utilized when there is a labor shortage or when a specialized need arises. The labor (or product) provided by the contractor must meet the organization's requirements also.

An *internal customer* is an employee of the company and a recipient of goods or services being provided by someone else who is an employee of the company. Just as the warehouse associate in the previous example is an internal supplier for the technicians, the technician is an internal customer for the warehouse associate. Who is the *external customer* in this example? The consumer who does not work for the organization and is the recipient of the service installation provided by the technician.

In between the input to the supplier and the output to the customer, there is a function called *system management* that ensures the desired level of quality and productivity. Work teams manage this system and ensure that it performs at optimum levels. Much of this work is done using the PROBE process model discussed in Chapter 6.

How the Facilitator Helps

In order to ensure the success of a team, the facilitator must attend to certain key areas. As the facilitator, you must interface with team members, suppliers, customers, and management whenever a new project is assigned to the team or whenever the team recognizes a new business need. There are several important guidelines that must be followed.

First, develop a written statement that identifies the problem, purpose, or need for a team. Include the following elements: clear definition of the problem or need, a description of the expected business payoff, and an estimate of the resources and time frame required.

Next, present the formal recommendation to management for approval. Identify management restrictions, determine how management wants to be kept informed of the team's progress, and clarify how much authority the team has.

> **Raison d'Etre**
>
> The facilitator should help in making a business case for a team's work because team members must justify their existence.

Management will assign one of three levels of authority to a specific team. These levels can be established on a project-by-project basis, or one level can be established for all projects assigned to a particular team. It is very important that a team understands its level, so that members can work comfortably within the boundaries. As the facilitator, discuss the team's authority level with management to help management decide and verbalize just how far the team can go.

The first level of authority is called *Level 1: Full Empowerment* or *post-updating*. This level is present when the team has full decision-making authority in reaching the established goal and updates the boss as decisions are carried out.

As an example, imagine that a team is assigned the task of eliminating all mechanical failures in its vehicle maintenance program. The team has the authority to do whatever is necessary to make this happen, with no approval from anyone. It must stay within its current departmental budget, but the group has full authority in deciding how it will reach its objective. It must keep upper management updated on current activity, but can go ahead with any decision made without management approval.

Customer Pursuit

Years ago, I managed a group of trainers in human resources at Food Giant, Inc. The level of authority I assigned this group was full empowerment. They kept me informed, but they did whatever they felt was needed to train all the hourly employees in the retail supermarkets. They decided to reinforce all of the training skills that were being taught with a company-wide game called Customer Pursuit.

There were competitions in each store, then district competitions, and finally a corporate competition in which the winners were given a vacation trip for two. Not only did my trainers reinforce the learning principles that were taught in the training programs, they also sent the message that learning could be fun. The whole project was hatched, designed, and implemented by the trainers, not by me. Yet, my contribution was allowing them to do what they felt was necessary. This is an example of how Level 1 can allow a group to make a significant impact on the welfare of an organization.

The second level of authority is called *Level 2: Management Approval* or *pre-approval*. This second level occurs when the team presents its recommendations for management approval after it has made a decision, and waits for a response before carrying out any plans. Using the previous example of teams trying to eliminate mechanical failures, Level 2 requires that the team present its recommendation for improvement to management. Management will review the recommendation and give the team authority to implement its recommendation, or possibly negotiate changes to the plan.

The third level of authority is called *Level 3: Management Decision* or *no authority*. In this situation, the team presents ideas for management to consider; it does not make the final decision. At this level, the team has virtually no authority. It simply presents its ideas to management. Management can either implement the team's plan or choose another course of action. This is the least desirable level of empowerment for a team. Try to convince management to avoid this mode because it negates one of the important benefits of work teams: ownership and dedication to the business.

Once the level of authority is established, the next step is to identify the boundaries. First of all, get approval for the resources the team needs, such as the number of people needed to work on the team, the necessary budget to achieve the goal, and any equipment needed to pursue the team's objective. Next, negotiate the schedule, including deadlines, for achieving the team's objective. An agreement on how much the team must produce to justify its existence is also important, as well as a description of the specific area the team must focus on.

If you are forming a new team, define its structure. This is done after approval for forming the team has been received. Plans should be made for how the team will be organized if it is coming together for the first time. Determine the follow-

Team Size Matters

Keep in mind that the optimum number of team members on any given team is six to 12 people. A team that is too small may limit its creative potential, while a team that is too big may be too cumbersome to work well.

ing functions:

- ▶ Identify to whom the team will report.
- ▶ Identify influential people who can give support to the group.
- ▶ Identify stakeholders, those who will be affected by the team's decisions and need to be kept informed.
- ▶ Develop a plan for selecting team members.
- ▶ Identify roles, responsibilities, and qualifications of team members.
- ▶ Decide who will educate, coach, and train the team if and when needed.

The *Initial Team Planning Form*, shown in Figure 8-2, can be used to assist you in organizing a new team. This can also be used to organize and publish the necessary information to keep the appropriate people informed.

Figure 8-2. Initial Team Planning Form

1. Specific problem/need _____
   _____

2. Customer needs related to this situation _____
   _____

3. Expected business payoff _____
   _____

4. Appropriate empowerment level: ____ Level 1 (Post-updating)
                                    ____ Level 2 (Pre-approval)
                                    ____ Level 3 (None)

5. Team structure: Facilitator _____

                         Reports to _____

   Team member responsibilities _____
   _____
   _____

   Selection process to begin on: _____ First group meeting: _____
   Team member qualifications _____
   _____

   Those who can give support _____
   _____

   Stakeholders to be kept informed _____
   _____

   Trainer/coach for the group _____
   _____

   Project deadline _____
   How often the team will meet _____

Team Development Stages

Once a temporary or permanent team has been formed and is working on its first project, it will develop and grow through four different stages: forming, storming, norming, and performing.

The forming phase occurs as team members get to know one another and bond with one another. Individuals react quite differently from each other in this phase. Some are very eager to jump into the project, while others take a more reluctant approach. Usually, team members display an initial politeness with one another. As the team begins to work together, things may appear to be progressing quite nicely. Initial friendships are often positive, and the team performs fairly well at this stage. This atmosphere usually changes as the team members work together more extensively and the newness of the situation wears off.

The forming phase occurs as team members get to know one another and bond with one another.

The Growth Phases

The facilitator must understand each of the four phases of growth and be able to identify which phase a team is in. Once a particular phase has been identified, the facilitator can then help the team be more effective in that particular stage and prepare for the next one. These stages should be used as a guide, since every team or group does not fit into a predictable pattern. Team members often find themselves going through the stages of development at different times. In other words, a team that has moved into the performing phase might still return to the storming phase at times.

What can the facilitator do to help a team in the *forming stage*? The facilitator must help the team get past the initial politeness and discomfort that exists in a new environment. This will clear the way for more serious issues to surface. The facilitator should help the team clarify sources of discomfort by asking questions. For example: "I noticed some head-shaking when we discussed what our time frame should be for this project. Do we need to discuss the deadline further?"

During formation, team members may also tend to focus on one another's differences without recognizing how to capitalize on them. You can encourage the team to use its diversity to its advantage. Teams must utilize all members to reach their full potential. In addition, you can point out the common goal that members have and ask them how they plan to work with their differences. You might say, "This team represents a lot of diverse talent, which will be particularly helpful in reaching our objective of increasing revenue opportunities with our new product. What are your suggestions for fully utilizing the talent in this room?"

As the team develops, members move into the *storming phase*. Due to disagreements and disparities regarding how the team is operating, conflicts may arise. Groups don't always deal with this effectively. Conflict and disagreement should be allowed to surface and be resolved—and the facilitator can help make this happen. Chapter 5 discussed how groups or teams deal with conflict and how the facilitator can help manage it.

A team must go through this storming phase in order to continue to grow and develop. Conflict usually occurs early on because group members have not yet had an opportunity to reach a consensus on the best ways to work together. Conflict provides them with opportunities to decide how to work together effectively and move to the next phase. As differences and tensions surface, the facilitator should allow and encourage discussion of these differences. If the discussion becomes destructive,

> ## No Two Are Alike
> Much of the dynamics that take place within a team are usually unpredictable. If you have an opportunity to work with several different teams, you'll find that no two teams are alike.

with team members making personal attacks, the facilitator must step in and remind the group that this is not acceptable. Encourage them to focus on the issues, not the people. The group will move through the storming phase only if the facilitator constantly encourages a discussion of the issues: "Let's remember that we're discussing how these errors occurred and what can be done to prevent them. We've agreed that personal attacks are not constructive and certainly won't help anyone reach an agreement on this issue. Lynn, continue explaining your plan for correcting this problem ...."

In the *norming phase*, the team begins to experience authentic success in working toward its objectives. People have identified behaviors that, if displayed consistently, help members work together effectively. These accepted behaviors, called *group norms*, have been discovered as a result of the difficulties experienced in phase two. Team members have learned what works best for them. Examples of group norms are:

In the norming phase, *the team begins to experience authentic success in working toward its objectives.*

- ▶ Allow each person who is speaking to finish without being interrupted.

- ▶ Give dissenters a chance to express their views. Hear them out, then strive for consensus.

121

▶ Silence means consent. If someone doesn't speak out against an idea, it will be assumed that everyone agrees with it.

▶ Make a concerted effort to listen and understand others' ideas, even if you don't agree.

▶ Stay on schedule—finish projects within the agreed-upon time frame.

There are two types of norms that emerge in this phase: *inherent norms* and *overt norms*. *Inherent norms* are natural behavioral tendencies that occur automatically and help the team maintain its effectiveness. *Overt norms* are behaviors that the team learns. Not all norms are positive, but team members should work toward using the positive norms and avoiding the ones that make it difficult for them to be successful together. Positive inherent and overt norms should become second nature as the group recognizes how they help the team be more effective.

The *Team Mission/Objective Form* in Figure 8-3 can be used to help develop positive overt norms by clarifying why the team exists, what it's responsible for, and how they will work together. A facilitator can use this form to help a group reach agreement on these elements.

The *performing phase* is the ultimate development phase for a team. This phase is characterized by strong bonds and good rapport among team members. All team members stand ready and willing to help one another in reaching their objectives. The group is very independent, and it responds automatically to any challenges or issues that arise.

A mature, performing team can accomplish quite a bit. It has experienced conflict and knows how to manage it. Team members have made commitments on how they will support each other and work together, and consis-

---

Working Together Effectively

In order to help the team recognize the most effective means of working together, the facilitator should point out both the inherent and overt norms of behavior that seem to work well or are needed. The most important ones can be added to the ground rules as a constant reminder of how to work together effectively.

Praising the team's productiveness and encouraging the team to solve problems when difficulties do arise will help the team become more independent. The facilitator should challenge team members to rely on themselves to accomplish goals, work out conflicts, and become a cohesive unit.

> ### Figure 8-3. Team Mission/Objective Form
> ▶ Who are our customers?
> ▶ Who are our suppliers?
> ▶ Why does our team exist?
> ▶ How do we contribute to our company's mission and vision?
> ▶ What specific tasks are we responsible for?
> ▶ What authority level do we have?
> ▶ What are our ground rules for working together effectively?
> ▶ What are our ground rules for resolving conflict?
> ▶ What are our ground rules for length, frequency, and location of our meetings?

tently adhere to these commitments. Teams in this phase have a great sense of pride in what they have accomplished and in their potential for future success.

The facilitator should serve as the catalyst for movement toward continuous improvement for a performing team. Since the team members share a common vision in this phase, they will be able to initiate many of their own projects based upon priorities. The facilitator becomes the team's advisor by pointing out areas where additional improvements in the process could be made. Since the performing team experiences a large amount of success, the facilitator has many opportunities to encourage members, reinforce a job well done, and praise the group.

The facilitator should serve as the catalyst for movement toward continuous improvement for a performing team.

Chapter Summary:
Helping Teams Be Successful

This chapter has identified how to form a team and create an environment that helps a team maintain success. The definition of a team is a group of people that work together and who have been given the authority to solve problems and address opportunities in the business.

The Realities of Teams

Teams work on increasing production, reducing errors, and eliminating waste. They should be brought together when the situation requires more than one person, contains more than one possible solution, and allows enough time for the team to address it.

There are two types of teams—permanent teams, which have been created for an indefinite amount of time, and temporary teams, which are created to work on special projects that have a beginning date and an ending date. Team members can be functional (same job, similar skills), cross-functional (different skills and jobs, same work process), and multi-functional (same skills, all know all steps of a work process).

How the Facilitator Helps

The facilitator helps teams perform in a number of ways. He or she develops written statements to identify the objective, the business payoff, and the estimate of resources. The facilitator also clarifies which level of authority the team will be assigned: Level 1, 2, or 3. The facilitator is responsible for acquiring the needed resources and the necessary budget as well as negotiating deadlines for accomplishing the specified goal. The Initial Team Planning Form is a good tool for identifying what needs to be done.

The facilitator helps the team grow and develop through the four stages of team growth. Team members need to be candid and learn to value each other's differences in the forming stage. Conflict and disagreement should be allowed to surface in the storming stage. The facilitator should help the team identify the most appropriate behaviors for success in the norming stage. For a performing team, the facilitator serves as a catalyst for continued improvement.

Chapter 9

What if I'm Not the Facilitator?

Natalie: I'm not going to be at the staff meeting today. I have a meeting with a customer.
Joseph: Well, the staff meeting is required. Helena expects everyone to be there.
Natalie: I don't get it. Week after week, those meetings are a waste! We never get anything done.

It's stressful to be in a meeting that isn't going anywhere when there are so many other things that you need to do. If you are conducting a meeting, you can control the quality of it. But what if you're just a participant? What can you do to impact the progress of a meeting?

As a participant, you have more influence than you may realize. It's not necessary to tolerate fruitless meetings, especially those that take up a significant amount of precious time. But you have to be committed to speak up when a meeting needs help. Most people are happy to complain quietly when a meeting is ineffective. But there is seldom a genuine effort toward making any improvement. It takes courage to verbalize a concern about a meeting's progress.

Why do people hesitate to complain publicly about ineffective or unnecessary meetings? Because there is a certain implied risk that goes along with it.

This is especially true when the person responsible for conducting the meeting is someone at a higher level. Unsolicited negative feedback may put one's job or position at risk.

Another reason people don't like complaining publicly is because it's challenging to say something negative in a tactful way. The recipient of the negative comment might get defensive and not appreciate the constructive feedback.

This chapter will help you meet the challenges of influencing the course of ineffective meetings that you attend but do not facilitate. First, this chapter will examine the importance of taking a position and standing behind it. Then, we will discuss the three levels of feedback and when to apply them. You'll receive specific guidelines on how to give feedback when you notice a meeting is not going well.

Be Willing to Speak Out

In order to influence the progress of a meeting, you first must be willing to speak out.

In order to influence the progress of a meeting, you first must be willing to speak out. By not speaking out when you have a concern, you are saying, "I am willing to live with what's happening here, even though it is a waste of time." Then, you must accept the results of a poorly run meeting: mediocre decisions, poor communication, and poor company performance.

Being willing to speak out is important in many areas. I recall a trip I took to New Orleans. I went with a group of friends for a long weekend. Everyone took turns driving the van we rented. One evening, on our way to a restaurant, one person decided it was her turn to drive. She was in a giddy mood, which suddenly began to affect her driving. She was joking around and not keeping her eyes on the road. When she sped up and started swerving, everyone got quiet.

I didn't want to say anything to her. I knew it would be embarrassing. But I also didn't want to be in an accident. So I pointed out that she should slow down. Immediately, someone else agreed. That's all we needed to say, because she immediately apologized and slowed down. If I hadn't said anything, I would have sent the unspoken message that her driving was OK with me. And I might have had to live with some dire consequences.

When you decide against trying to influence the quality of a meeting, you also have to live with the consequences. First, an ineffective meeting wastes time. It prevents you from accomplishing something of value, which could impact your job performance. In addition to the waste of time, poor meetings typically result in mediocre decisions, with little or no commitment to carrying out those decisions. So, nothing ever seems to get done. This mediocre pattern often grows, affecting bottom-line company performance.

Three Ways to Speak Out

You may be wondering how you can actually make a positive difference in influencing the quality of a meeting. The *way* you do this is just as important as deciding to do it. Whatever you say or do needs to be well received by the person responsible for the meeting. There are three levels of action to choose from. I like the first two:

▶ Pebbles

▶ Rocks

▶ Boulders

You may be wondering how you can actually make a positive difference in influencing the quality of a meeting. The way you do this is just as important as deciding to do it.

A *pebble* is a subtle, gentle action you would take to influence the quality of a meeting. You can often do this by asking a question.

For example, let's say that you're attending a meeting called to address a problem with a new software program being used by the company. After being in the meeting for 15 minutes, you are still not sure what the group is there to accomplish. So, at a break in the discussion, you say, "Before we go any further, I have a question. I understand your description of this problem, but what specifically do we want to accomplish during this meeting?" This one question can actually change the course of the meeting by ensuring that each participant is focused in the same direction.

A pebble is the easiest of the three actions you can take. And it often takes only one or two pebbles to make an impact. It is also the least risky of the three actions.

Let's say that you are in the middle of a meeting and you notice that the group has begun discussing something that is not on the agenda. You could say something like "Does this topic need to go on the parking lot for tomorrow's meeting?"

Pointed Questions

By pointing out your observations with a question, you give other group members an opportunity to validate what you've noticed.

This will often trigger a change during the meeting, one that will help everyone be more productive.

A *rock* is a very direct but appropriate action you take after you've already thrown some pebbles with no success. It's also used when you need to take immediate action due to the urgency of a situation.

A rock is a very direct but appropriate action you take after you've already thrown some pebbles with no success.

Imagine that someone who reports to you is planning to facilitate a meeting for a group of senior managers. As she is planning for the meeting, you notice that the agenda doesn't address the issue of most concern to the participants. You also realize you've had this problem with her in the past. You've thrown some pebbles with gentle reminders about being responsive to the group's needs, but she still often misses the group members' most important concerns.

This oversight compromises senior management support, which is critical

> ### Chapter 5 Rocks
>
> The interventions discussed in Chapter 5 are considered rocks. As discussed, they are used only after ineffective behavior has become a pattern. Pebbles, or gentle reminders, are always used first, even when conducting a meeting.

in meeting departmental objectives. This time, you use the process for one-on-one interventions, discussed in Chapter 5. Rather than reminding her about this group's specific concern, you begin the discussion around her inability to hear the most important concerns of a group. You use this specific agenda as an example. Discuss the negative impact and ask how she could become more effective.

Another example of a rock can be found in a situation I found myself in recently. I was asked to facilitate a meeting by a senior marketing manager of a telecommunications company. I was expected to help the group meet specific objectives during the meeting.

> ### The Rock
>
> Delivering a rock is mentally challenging, but you gain respect when you deliver one that is needed.

Once the meeting started, the senior manager became more and more domineering. Other people in the room stopped participating. She began taking over my job as facilitator and trying to push the group toward a specific direction in which only she wanted to go. I called a break and talked with her privately about this, using the process for a one-on-one intervention. She immediately backed off and allowed me to continue. The situation called for immediate action because I wanted to facilitate a productive meeting. You sometimes must be directive in your approach to change a situation that needs addressing. That's exactly what I did with this senior manager. We were running out of time, so the situation called for me to be direct.

You might be saying to yourself, "A rock is pretty risky with someone who is senior to me. I don't know if I could do that." You must weigh the risks and ultimately make the judgment. If you've already tried several pebbles, a rock is appropriate. If you need to take immediate action, a rock is also appropriate. You have to quickly assess the person you're dealing with and decide the level of risk. Here are some less risky approaches:

1. Get several individuals to approach the person separately.
2. Convince the entire group to approach the person as a group, taking care to communicate concerns tactfully.
3. Talk with someone who is influential with the person and would be willing to talk with him or her.

A *boulder* is rarely if ever recommended. It is defined as a very forceful, blunt action that is taken to direct a meeting in a particular way. You know you've thrown a boulder when the person receiving it is offended or even shattered by your approach. If the recipient of your message is more focused on *how* you verbalized your concern and less interested in *what* your concern is, you've probably thrown a boulder.

A boulder is rarely if ever recommended. It is defined as a very forceful, blunt action that is taken to direct a meeting in a particular way.

To avoid throwing boulders, refrain from:

1. Blurting out what you want to say
2. Calling names
3. Letting your tone of voice express impatience, anger, irritation, or condescension

Three Opportunities

Pebbles or rocks should be thrown at the appropriate moments:

1. When you receive information about an upcoming meeting
2. When you are attending a meeting
3. When you have just completed a meeting

You may see red flags even before the meeting starts. Each of these red flags might signal the need for a pebble or a rock in order to help change the course of the upcoming meeting.

▶ The wrong people have been invited.

▶ There is no clear purpose for the meeting.

▶ The attached agenda does not seem to support the meeting's purpose.

▶ There is no starting or ending time.

▶ A meeting really isn't needed.

If you know enough about the meeting's subject matter to determine that the wrong people have been invited, your tactful comments might be appreciated. Remember to always use a facilitative approach. You could say something like "Bob Carson's area of expertise is in programming. Does he need to be at this meeting?" This might force the person who sent out the meeting notice to at least re-examine the list of participants.

If you know enough about the meeting's subject matter to determine that the wrong people have been invited, your tactful comments might be appreciated.

When you do not detect a clear purpose, agenda, or start and end times, you'll find it quite comfortable to ask about it: "Could you explain the purpose of our meeting so that I can make sure I'm prepared for it? An agenda would also be helpful for my own preparation." You could address the starting and ending times by asking for them so that you can block the meeting off on your calendar.

All of these suggestions are pebbles, which is where you should always start. A rock is appropriate only when you've already tried several pebbles. If the pebbles haven't made a significant ripple, assess the situation and decide if it's safe to throw a rock. You couldn't tell your boss to include an agenda for the upcoming meeting, but you could tell one of your direct reports to do so.

You also want to be careful about announcing that a scheduled meeting isn't really needed and that it would be just as effective to send out an e-mail or phone message. But you could ask if, because of your busy schedule, you could use an alternative to attending the scheduled meeting: "Would it be possible for you to send us an e-mail on this instead of having a meeting?" If the answer is "No," then you must decide if the situation is safe enough to throw a rock: "Well, unfortunately, I can't make it. I promised to meet with a customer. I'll plan to get together with you after the meeting to discuss this subject."

There are several signs to watch for when you are attending a meeting. These signs are opportunities for you to influence and improve the meeting's progress:

1. The group has gotten off the agenda item that it is supposed to be addressing.

2. The meeting is behind schedule or has gone past the scheduled ending time.
3. There is no clear purpose or agenda.
4. The person conducting the meeting isn't helping and seems to be hampering progress.
5. There is little open communication.
6. Several members are silent.
7. Participants are doing a lot of interrupting and little listening.

When you have just finished attending a meeting, there may also be an opportunity to give feedback to the facilitator. This is especially true if you are asked to do so. But you could also tactfully make some helpful suggestions. Here are some behaviors and situations you could comment on, if you observe them:

1. The facilitator has trouble keeping the group focused.
2. There is very little group participation.
3. One or two group members remain silent.
4. The facilitator is getting resistance from group members.
5. The agenda does not lead the group to the stated outcome.
6. The facilitator is having trouble leading the group toward consensus.

In any of the above situations, you should have your suggestions ready if you are going to point them out to the facilitator. The facilitator will most likely be aware of the difficulty and might appreciate your ideas. Just be sure to give them in a supportive manner. Figure 9-1 suggests areas to focus on if a meeting seems to be in trouble. These suggestions may help in the challenging situations mentioned above.

Figure 9-1. Where to Focus if a Meeting Is in Trouble

Difficult Situation	Solution/Prevention
1. The facilitator has trouble keeping the group focused	Is there an outcome? Is the agenda being followed? Is the facilitator asking the group to stay focused? Is a parking lot being used?
2. There is very little group participation	Are group members intimidated? Has the facilitator encouraged participation? Is there one dominating individual the facilitator needs to deal with?

(Continued on next page)

Figure 9-1. Where to Focus if a Meeting Is in Trouble

Difficult Situation	Solution/Prevention
3. There are one or two group members who are silent	Are all group members encouraged to give input? Has the facilitator addressed the silent members individually, in private?
4. The facilitator is getting resistance from group members	What is causing the resistance? Has the facilitator addressed the reason for resistance? Is the facilitator being content neutral? Is the facilitator making it easy or difficult for the group to achieve the meeting outcome?
5. The agenda does not lead the group to the stated outcome	Was the outcome written before the agenda was written?
6. The facilitator is having trouble leading the group toward consensus	Is everyone listening effectively? Has the facilitator ensured that all opposing parties understand each other? Has the facilitator placed responsibility for reaching consensus upon the group?

(Continued from previous page)

Chapter Summary:
Problem Solving as a Meeting Participant

As a participant, you can positively influence the quality of a meeting. You must first be willing to speak out. When you decide against giving constructive suggestions, you are saying, "I am going to tolerate the poor quality of this meeting and the mediocre decisions that result."

There are three levels of action that you can take to influence the progress of a meeting. Using a pebble is the easiest and least risky. You point out what you're observing by asking a question such as "Have we gotten off track?" A rock is more direct, but still appropriate. It's used to make statements and suggestions about what you're observing. There is more risk with a rock, so you must use judgment to weigh the risks and decide how to present your suggestion. A boulder is never recommended. It's too blunt to ever make a positive impact on the recipient of your feedback.

There are three opportunities for which to use pebbles and rocks:

▶ Before a meeting

▶ During a meeting

▶ After a meeting

Look for red flags that signal a potential problem, such as:

▶ There is no clear purpose or agenda.

▶ The wrong people are invited.

▶ The group is off track.

▶ The group is not following the agenda.

▶ There is very little participation.

When you notice a red flag, this is your opportunity! You can choose to ignore the problem or act to solve the problem. Your meetings will vastly improve when you decide to voice your observations.

Chapter 10

Test Yourself

N ow that you have read about the skills needed for managing a meeting and a group, it's time to apply them to the real-life scenarios described in this chapter.

How would you handle each of these difficult situations if you were the facilitator? First, write your answer on a separate sheet of paper. Then, review the appropriate response following each of these cases.

Case Situations

Case One

You are facilitating a group of managers for a major automobile manufacturer. Jim has brought up an important issue—how to improve production time. Members are trying to estimate how much production time can be decreased for each of the alternatives they are considering. Mary introduces a new subject, the design for one of next year's models, and wants to discuss it in detail.

Case One Response

Ask Mary if the new subject could be listed on the parking lot sheet, to be addressed later. You might say, "Right now, we're discussing ways to improve production time. In order to stay focused, could we add this new subject to the parking lot to be addressed later?"

Case Two

You are working with a group of information technology support managers from a medium-sized long-distance company. They are clarifying a list of new services for their internal customers. As group members begin to clarify the list that has just been created, Delores, a very persuasive team member, begins to discuss how well the fifth option would work. She likes this option because several of her customers have recommended it.

Case Two Response

Ask Delores to hold her comments until after the group has finished clarifying all of the options: "Delores, could you please hold your comments about that? Let's finish clarifying these options to make sure everyone understands them. Then, I'll come back to you when we start evaluating." But don't forget to get back to Delores!

Case Three

You are facilitating a group from a lending institution that is discussing how to introduce a new equity accelerator program. Your group consists of several members with different job positions, representing a cross-section of bank employees. Nato, a loan officer, makes a suggestion that no one else in the group acknowledges. You sense that the others don't like the idea.

Case Three Response

Allow all suggestions to be addressed, even if the group doesn't like a particular idea. Offer specific guidance: "What about Nato's suggestion? What are your thoughts?" Help the group fully consider all suggestions before it determines which options are best. You also protect the self-esteem of group members by ensuring that all ideas are heard. This encourages participation from all members.

Case Four

A group of retail store managers is planning a big product promotion for an upcoming holiday. James is discussing an idea he has, but is interrupted by

Joey, who enthusiastically jumps into the discussion.

Case Four Response

When one group member interrupts another, simply say, "Joey, hold on—let's wait for James to finish and we'll hear your comment next." It is common for group members to interrupt each other. By reminding them to listen to the entire message before interrupting, you set a precedent for good communication skills among group members. You also encourage members to stay involved in the conversation. Remember to get Joey's input next.

Case Five

Your group is from a brokerage company and they are brainstorming ideas for a new financial product. There is a lot of energy and excitement during this portion of the meeting. Two people, Annette and Nick, start talking at the same time. Annette "wins out" and is able to thoroughly discuss her idea.

Case Five Response

After Annette is finished, go to Nick, who started to talk, but did not get a chance to share his views: "Nick, did you start to say something?" Some group members will not offer a comment after being cut off. You can provide encouragement by calling on those who want to say something, but need an opening in the discussion to do so.

Case Six

You are facilitating a group from a small accounting firm. They are planning a retirement party for one of their senior members. Nina is explaining her suggestion to the rest of the group. She talks for quite some time and appears to be rambling. You notice that some of the other group members, especially Rita and Michael, are becoming impatient and are ready to move on.

Case Six Response

When Nina takes a breath or pauses, try paraphrasing what she has said, then check to be sure the group understands what she is saying: "So, what you're saying is …. Is that right? Good. Does everyone understand what Nina is saying? Then are we ready to move on?" Group members sometimes need help in expressing themselves. If you are listening effectively, you can draw out the ideas being expressed so that everyone is understood.

Case Seven

You work in a children's hospital. The meeting you are facilitating involves a group of human resources specialists. They are creating a plan for rolling out a new training program. As the group is discussing an issue, a sidebar conversation begins between Frank and Rebecca. It becomes distracting to the rest of the group, but the two group members are not aware of this.

Case Seven Response

Whenever there is a prolonged sidebar conversation in which some members of a group begin to discuss matters on their own, you should address it tactfully, by saying something like "Let's remember to focus on what's going on so we don't miss anything." If the sidebar continues, talk to the individuals privately during a break: "I'm noticing that you are having a number of sidebar conversations. Has either of you noticed this?" Give them time to discuss it. Then try to help them recognize the impact. If they can't, explain that private conversations can be distracting for the group. Then ask, "What can you do to avoid these sidebar conversations?" Be ready to offer a suggestion, such as sharing valid comments with everyone else.

Case Eight

You are facilitating a group of high school principals. They are working on ideas for a new curriculum focusing on history. Connie is making a suggestion and is having trouble expressing her thoughts accurately—she is searching for the right words. Bob tries to help by rephrasing the suggestion.

Case Eight Response

Make sure that Bob, who is trying to help, is accurately rephrasing the other person's message. Ask Connie to confirm: "Connie, is that what you were saying?" It is important to capture the exact thoughts of the person contributing the idea, so there is no misunderstanding about what the person wants to say.

Case Nine

You are working with a group of engineers from a gas company. The group is 20 minutes into the meeting. You notice that two members, Lynn and Alberta, haven't said anything yet.

Case Nine Response

Pull in silent members tactfully and gently: "Let's hear from someone who has not had a chance to express their opinion on this. Do you have anything to add?" If this doesn't help, then you can directly ask a silent member, "Lynn, have you had a chance to formulate an opinion yet?"

Silent group members may have reasons for being silent. They could have serious concerns about the topic being discussed or they may not have formed an opinion yet. Sometimes members are naturally quiet and introverted. It is important to ask for their involvement tactfully, so they are not singled out.

Case Ten

You are facilitating a group of automobile dealers that has already met three times. They are sharing ideas on how to promote loyalty in customers. You notice that one person, Pete, never speaks or contributes any ideas. You've called on him a few times to ask for his input, but he never has anything to say.

Case Ten Response

Since you have already called on Pete several times during the group meetings and he is still not participating, it is time to do an intervention to change behavior. Talk with him during the break or outside the meeting in private: "Pete, you are silent most of the time during meetings. Are you conscious of this or are you normally quiet?" Give him time to express his views. Then ask, "How do you think this impacts you?" If he doesn't know, explain that the group is missing out on his expertise and may perceive him as uninterested in the project. Next, you should ask, "What could you do to be more active and involved?" If he doesn't have any ideas, be prepared to offer your own: "If we are discussing an area that you know something about, just raise your hand and I'll make sure you have a chance to contribute. I'll also be calling on you more often to give you more opportunities to speak." You have now discussed the situation with Pete and have clearly told him you expect him to participate more.

Some people are normally quiet and are more comfortable contributing in other ways. It's possible for an individual to be engaged without being extremely vocal. You may need to help a quiet member find alternative ways to be involved.

Case 11

You are facilitating a group of corporate lawyers who work for a large telecommunications company. You notice that one group member, Rita, is doing all the talking during the meeting.

Case 11 Response

This is challenging: the dominating, overly vocal individual! You cannot ignore Rita, because the problem will reflect on you if you do not handle it. First, try to be subtle and make broad statements to pull in other people: "Well, we heard from Rita. Let's hear from someone else. What are your ideas about this?"

If Rita does not take the hint after you have tried this a few times, then you must talk to her privately and make an intervention. Tell her, "Rita, your participation is excellent and I'd like to extend participation to more people. How could we do that?" Discuss some ideas and agree on the best approach.

Case 12

A group of customer service managers is trying to identify performance standards for their customer service reps in a call center. You have been facilitating their discussion. There seem to be two opposing viewpoints. Sheila, Ron, Laura, and Sarah think that the reps should be able to handle at least 100 calls per day. Jay, John, Matt, and Jessica believe the reps should be encouraged to spend more time with each caller, thereby reducing the daily number of calls to only 75. They have been debating this subject for 20 minutes.

Case 12 Response

First of all, remind the group of the amount of time that has been allotted for the meeting and what has been planned for the rest of the agenda. Ask members if they want to continue discussing this issue or would rather think about it and address it later. If the group decides to continue discussing it, list the opposing points of view in outline form on the easel. Then, ask the group members to point out areas of agreement and disagreement, as you write them on the flip chart. You can then ask them to develop a solution that all of them could support.

Case 13

You have been facilitating a group who works in a power plant. The meeting has been in session for one hour. The group members are trying to develop a plan for outages. One member, John, falls asleep.

Case 13 Response

If a group member is sleeping, call a break. He or she may just need a cup of coffee or a soda. If the problem continues, address it one on one and find out why the person is sleeping: "John, you are the subject-matter expert on this project. You have the knowledge and experience that the group needs. When you fall asleep, this gives the group the impression that you simply don't care about the project. I'd like to discuss why you're sleeping and what can be done to keep you awake." Be ready to suggest, if John cannot think of any solutions, that he drink coffee or stand up in the back of the room when he gets sleepy. If he is able to explain why he is falling asleep, this could give you some additional ideas for helping him solve the problem.

Case 14

You are facilitating a team of salespeople in a software company. They have been charged with identifying prospective customers in new markets. Team members have indicated that they don't want to be a team. Several members, including Elizabeth, Angelique, Thomas, and Rick, do not feel that the company has demonstrated real support for their efforts.

Case 14 Response

Ask the members why they feel this way. Build a list of actions that management could take to give the group support. Offer to present it to management or ask the members if they would like to select someone from the team to present it. If they do not want to approach management, then encourage them to list ways they can operate, given the current situation. If this does not work, then you might consider sitting down with management and talking about the situation. Bring a recommendation for resolving the issue.

The discussion with management should go something like this: "This team has a lot of talent and initiative, so they will require little supervision on this project. However, they feel that they are not getting the outside support they need to get the job done effectively. I suggest you meet with the members and hear what their needs are for this project. Once they understand that they have the support they need, they will be able to refocus their energies to meet their objectives. How does this sound to you?"

Case 15

You are facilitating a meeting for a group of district managers who work for a grocery chain. They are forecasting sales for the upcoming quarter. The group's manager, Vince, is dominating the group and taking too much control of the discussion.

Case 15 Response

Even bosses and managers need feedback, but it should be offered in private. You might ask Vince to limit his comments so the group does not feel pressure to follow his lead, since the purpose of the meeting is to gain input from district managers. You might say, "It's clear this issue is important to you and your belief in the project is important to the group. However, your involvement in the discussion makes it difficult for the rest of the group members to participate. They become more hesitant. What can you do to show your enthusiasm and still allow the others to contribute?"

If Vince has no ideas, tell him, "I suggest you refrain from contributing your opinions. Simply praise the group for their hard work and support them by offering whatever they need to accomplish their task."

Appendix A

The Case of Cable Express Inc.

Y ou've now read about all the principles for conducting effective meetings, solving problems, and leading groups in an organized manner. You've also evaluated situations that typically arise for facilitators. Hopefully, you have already begun to put these principles into action.

This appendix will give you an opportunity to review these principles. You will be reading about a fictitious cable company called Cable Express. The company has a few operational problems that are impacting its customers. You will see how a facilitator might typically help a management team choose the most pressing problem to focus on first, and then define the problem, identify the root cause of the problem, and develop options for solving the problem.

Cable Express Inc.: A Thumbnail Sketch of a Company

Cable Express (CE) is a cable company with 45,000 residential customers. CE is based in a large city and is one of four cable companies that serve the city. CE is a medium-sized company in this market, but it is part of a nationwide cable organization with operations in 15 other states.

While Cable Express is backed by a large and successful parent company, all the company-owned systems are held to very stringent budgets, so resources, at times, can be limited. When extra funding is needed, it has to be approved by the home office.

Cable Express is experiencing several problems in its operations. First, the company is losing customers in a few areas. A competing cable company (owned by a telecommunications firm) is sending out door-to-door salespeople who are able to hook up cable instantly. Although this has occurred in only a few of CE's outlying areas, the company has lost approximately 45 percent of its customers in these markets. Several customers who decided to go with the competition stated that they were tired of waiting for Cable Express to hook them up. This is understandable, since CE customers currently experience a four-day wait.

Current customers are also having problems when they order additional services or request repair work. The wait time is even longer than for new customers—seven days. In addition, the company has received a very large number of customer complaints, focusing on such issues as billing errors, rude customer service reps, and poor picture quality with its cable service.

After meeting with his management team to discuss the issues, the general manager at CE, John Duffy, realizes his company needs the expertise of a facilitator to help them acquire some focus for addressing these challenges. He meets with several potential facilitators and decides on Natalie Simonson.

The First Meeting

In preparing for the first meeting, Natalie realizes from the initial discussion with John that there are several problems at CE. She knows that an organization with limited resources should focus on one major area at a time. Often this will result in other problems or issues being resolved as well. Also, it helps focus employees: they achieve results faster and are then motivated to tackle another area.

With this in mind, she develops the following outcome for the meeting: "a prioritized list of CE problems to be solved." Once the group has developed this list, it can tackle each problem one at a time. Now, Natalie is ready to develop an agenda.

During the "Beginning of the Meeting" phase, Natalie plans time for the group members to develop their own list of ground rules, since they will be meeting on an ongoing basis. Natalie will contract with the group by asking if everyone is willing to follow these ground rules for each of the meetings they will be attending.

For the "Body of the Meeting," she decides to use a portion of the PROBE process model—the O (Options) and B (Best Options) steps. Natalie plans to facilitate as the participants brainstorm a list of current problems that CE is experiencing. Next, the problems that need clarifying will be discussed to ensure everyone understands them. Finally, the group will use the multi-vote process tool to prioritize the list from most important to least important. (To review any of the process tools mentioned here, see Chapter 6.)

Natalie will end the meeting by summarizing, setting the next meeting date, and verifying any other action items that might have been discussed. She will close the meeting on a positive note by praising the group members on something they did that was especially effective.

After looking over the agenda she has developed (illustrated in Figure A-1), Natalie plans the meeting for approximately one and a half hours. This will give the group ample time to achieve the intended outcome and for her to answer any questions. (She's anticipating the participants will have questions, since this is their first meeting with her.) This agenda is for Natalie's eyes only (it has more detail than the group needs), so she will publish another agenda that has less detail and send it out to the participants in advance of the meeting (Figure A-2).

At the meeting, unnecessary truck rolls becomes the number-one priority on the list. A truck roll occurs whenever a technician drives from the warehouse to a customer's house to perform a service. An unnecessary truck roll occurs if a technician makes more than one trip to the customer's home when the service could have been provided in only one trip.

The company's key measurements concerning truck rolls indicate that each day 13 technicians visit approximately 150 customers. Meanwhile, there are 40 unnecessary trips back to the warehouse and then out again to the customer's house. So, instead of 150 visits, there are 190 visits. That means that 27 percent of the truck rolls are unnecessary. By solving this one problem, the managers realize they could dramatically reduce the amount of time it takes to hook up new customers and provide service for existing customers. This would reduce the amount of complaints they are getting about delayed service.

Figure A-1. Meeting Agenda for
Cable Express First Meeting

Expected Outcome: A prioritized list of CE problems to be solved
Date: 1/5
Time: 9:00 AM
Place: Conference room
Who Should Attend: F. Catalfamo, J. Duffy, A. Franklin, T. Hoff, L. King,
M. Kensey, J. Mewing, L. Little, B. Moss, L. Palma
R. Polly, R. Ringer

What	Time	Who
Beginning of the Meeting		
Welcome the group	5 minutes	
Clarify the outcome	5 minutes	
Set role expectations	5 minutes	
Establish ground rules		
a. Brainstorm a list of ground rules		
b. Clarify the list		
c. Contract with the group	20 minutes	
Discuss agenda	5 minutes	
Body of the Meeting		
Brainstorm possible causes	15 minutes	
Clarify the problems that need further explanation	10 minutes	
Prioritize the list using multi-vote	15 minutes	
Verify the first problem to work on	5 minutes	
End of the Meeting		
Summarize against the outcome	1 minute	
Verify action items, set next meeting date	1 minute	
Praise the group's effort	1 minute	

The Second Meeting

Now, Natalie is ready to prepare for her second meeting. She will apply the PROBE model to the problem of unnecessary truck rolls. The second session will require more thought and preparation from Natalie. The group will begin with the P phase, Projection, which means it'll create a goal that defines the problem and describes to what extent the problem will be solved.

Figure A-2. Cable Express Agenda for Group Members to Use

Expected Outcome: A prioritized list of CE problems to be solved
Date: 1/5
Time: 9:00 AM
Place: Conference room
Who Should Attend: F. Catalfamo, J. Duffyt, A. Franklin, T. Hoff, L. King, M. Kensey, J. Mewing, L. Little, B. Moss, L. Palma, R. Polly, R. Ringer

What	Time	Who
Introduction	7 minutes	
Outcome		
Set role expectations		
Establish ground rules		
Brainstorm a list of ground rules	10 minutes	
Clarify the list		
Contract with the group		
Brainstorm a list of problems	15 minutes	
Clarify the problems	10 minutes	
Prioritize the list using multi-vote and choose one problem to work on	20 minutes	
Summarize, set next meeting date	3 minutes	

As part of her preparation, Natalie also needs to choose which tool from the R phase, Root Cause Analysis, is most appropriate. Since the problem is unnecessary truck rolls, it is important to find out what is causing this. Since there are probably several factors involved, a check sheet would be a good way to track both the causes and the number of occurrences.

The group may also later want to examine the entire work process, beginning with the customer placing a telephone order to a customer service representative and ending with a technician appearing at the customer's home to handle the order. A flowchart could be used for this analysis. However, since the chart could get very involved—and might dilute both the company resources and the group focus—Natalie decides to stick to the check sheet for now.

Natalie has identified two outcomes for this meeting. This session may take longer than the first, but the group is willing to set aside as much as three hours, if necessary. She plans for one and a half hours. The intended outcomes are "a goal statement for eliminating unnecessary truck rolls and a check sheet for tracking the causes of unnecessary truck rolls." Figure A-3 shows both of these outcomes as well as the agenda designed to achieve them.

Figure A-3. Meeting Agenda for Cable Express Second Meeting

Expected Outcome: A goal statement for eliminating unnecessary truck rols and a check sheet for tracking the causes of unnecessary truck rolls
Date: 1/12
Time: 9:00 AM
Place: Conference room
Who Should Attend: F. Catalfamo, J. Duffyt, A. Franklin, T. Hoff, L. King, M. Kensey, J. Mewing, L. Little, B. Moss, L. Palma, R. Polly, R. Ringer

What	Time	Who
Beginning of the Meeting		
Welcome the group	1 minute	
Clarify the outcome	5 minutes	
Set role expectations	1 minute	
Contract ground rules	30 seconds	
Discuss agenda	30 seconds	
Body of the Meeting		
Discussion with guest speaker	20 minutes	Paul Evans
Develop a goal statement phrase	30 minutes	
a. Ask for ideas to complete three phrases of a goal statement We will ... In a way that ... So that ...		
Develop a check sheet; R phase		
a. List causes of unnecessary truck rolls	15 minutes	
b. Decide who will collect the information	10 minutes	
c. Decide on the time period for collecting	5 minutes	
End of the Meeting		
Summarize against the outcome	30 seconds	
Verify action items, set next meeting date	30 seconds	
Praise the group's efforts	30 seconds	

Natalie develops the agenda to reflect what the group has to do to reach the two outcomes listed at the top. There is also a guest speaker for this meeting. Paul Evans will be present to discuss some potential causes the group might decide to track. Paul works in the corporate office and has helped some of the other CE cable systems with similar problems. The group wanted to ask him some questions, so Natalie sets aside some time on the agenda for Paul to speak to the group.

At the meeting, Natalie simply follows her agenda and applies her facilitation skills, focusing on helping group members clearly communicate their ideas about the issues. The goal statement they develop is "We will reduce unnecessary truck rolls from 21 percent to 5 percent in a way that maintains current budget levels and head count so that our workforce will be more productive and our customers will be more satisfied."

Figure A-4 shows the check sheet developed during the second meeting. The causes listed on the check sheet should be as detailed as possible, in order

Figure A-4. Check Sheet Developed at the Second Meeting

Unnecessary Truck Rolls
Week Ending _____

Causes	Number of Occurrences
Customer changed mind	
CSR recorded inaccurate information	
Warehouse didn't give correct parts or enough parts	
Incorrect address	
Could not find customer's house	
Truck called back due to higher priority	
Disorganized service technician	
Technician error the first time service was performed	
Customer wasn't home	
Customer wanted an additional service	
Other (please specify)	
Other	
Other	

to ultimately identify the exact causes that are contributing most to the problem. At this meeting, team members decide they will meet weekly to review check-sheet data from the previous week. Once they begin to notice trends, they will start to identify options for eliminating the causes that occur the most often.

Natalie explains that, after looking at the initial results, members may decide they need to gather more data before being able to determine the most frequent incidences of causes. The causes listed may not be specific enough. For example, if a major factor turns out to be technician's error the first time service was performed, they might decide to gather more information by finding out which technicians were causing errors. If there were only a few technicians making mistakes, they might need to focus only on those few technicians to correct the problem.

The group meets two more times to review the check-sheet results and identify any causes that need more research. This often occurs when involved with root cause analysis. The layers of the onion have to be peeled back, one after the other, until the root cause has been revealed. It often helps to ask the question, "Why?" For example, the CSR recorded inaccurate information about the customer's order. Why? Because the CSR did not know how to input that specific type of order. Why? Because the procedure for inputting that specific type of order is very complicated and many CSRs have trouble with it. By doing enough research to find out the *real* cause, the group will have a better chance of solving the problem.

The Fifth Meeting

In preparation for the fifth meeting, Natalie must assess what is currently happening and what the group will need to do next. They will be analyzing several weeks' worth of data, reported in weekly increments, on causes of unnecessary truck rolls. They are ready to identify the more significant causes and decide on what actions need to take place to eliminate those causes. Natalie will use the O and B phases of PROBE to guide the group. The outcomes for this meeting will be "a list of solutions for eliminating the main causes of unnecessary truck rolls and a decision on which solutions will be implemented." Figure A-5 shows the agenda that Natalie develops. The meeting will be one hour and 45 minutes long, including a break.

Figure A-5. Meeting Agenda for Cable Express Fifth Meeting

Expected Outcome: A list of solutions for eliminating the main causes of unnecessary truck rolls and a decision on which solutions will be implemented
Date: 2/2
Time: 9:00 AM
Place: Conference room
Who Should Attend: F. Catalfamo, J. Duffyt, A. Franklin, T. Hoff, L. King, M. Kensey, J. Mewing, L. Little, B. Moss, L. Palma, R. Polly, R. Ringer

What	Time	Who
Beginning of the Meeting		
Welcome the group	1 minute	
Clarify the outcome and overall goal	5 minutes	
Set role expectations	15 seconds	
Contract ground rules	15 seconds	
Discuss agenda	30 seconds	
Body of the Meeting		
Review check-sheet results	15 minutes	
a. Identify causes that occur most often		
List options; O phase		
a. Brainstorm list of solutions	15 minutes	
b. Clarify the list of solutions	10 minutes	
c. Combine similar solutions into one	10 minutes	
Break	**10 minutes**	
Choose best options; B phase		
a. Eliminate the obvious	5 minutes	
b. Multi-vote to narrow the list	15 minutes	
c. Decide on options to implement	15 minutes	
End of the Meeting		
Summarize against the outcome	1 minute	
Verify action items, set next meeting date	1 minute	
Praise the group's effort	1 minute	

During this fifth meeting, the group identifies three causes that seem to occur the most frequently, according to the check-sheet results:

▶ The customer wasn't home.

- ▶ The customer wanted an additional service and the technician had to reschedule the service call.
- ▶ The technician could not find the customer's house.

Although other causes still need attention, these three causes together contribute to 65 percent of all unnecessary truck rolls. Therefore, the group decides to concentrate on these first.

The group decides on several solutions to eliminate the three identified causes.

First, create an automated phone message to send to the customer the day before the scheduled service visit to remind the customer of the appointment and to specify the type of service to be performed. A phone number will be included for the customer to call if there are any changes to the order or if the customer wants to reschedule the appointment. This will ensure that the customer is home when the technician arrives to provide service.

Next, a dispatcher will call the customer when the technician is on the way to the customer's home. The dispatcher can make sure the customer is there, clarify directions to the residence, and verify the service to be performed. This action will confirm that the technician can find the residence and knows what type of service is needed before arriving there.

Also, to help technicians be prepared for the unexpected, they'll be given a specified amount of additional equipment to carry on the truck; an inventory system will be developed to keep track of it. If the customer wants any service in addition to what was scheduled, it can be done on the same visit. Two technicians will be designated for high-priority work and for delivering needed parts and equipment. In addition, they'll help if any additional service is needed that requires a lot of time.

Other solutions may be needed later, but the group decides to start with these and continue to track the truck rolls to review progress.

The Sixth Meeting

The group decides to meet within a few days of the fifth meeting, so Natalie prepares by developing an intended outcome and meeting agenda. She will be guiding the group through the last phase of PROBE—E, Execution. The process tool she will use is the action-plan time line. The intended outcome she develops is "an action-plan time line for implementing the solutions to reduce unnecessary truck rolls." Figure A-6 shows the agenda she will use to facilitate the group through the process. The meeting will be about two hours and 15 minutes, including a break.

Figure A-6. Meeting Agenda for Cable Express Sixth Meeting

Expected Outcome: An action-plan time line for implementing the solution to reduce unnecessary truck rolls
Date: 2/5
Time: 9:00 AM
Place: Conference room
Who Should Attend: F. Catalfamo, J. Duffyt, A. Franklin, T. Hoff, L. King, M. Kensey, J. Mewing, L. Little, B. Moss, L. Palma, R. Polly, R. Ringer

What	Time	Who
Beginning of the Meeting		
Welcome the group	15 seconds	
Clarify the outcome and overall goal	10 minutes	
Set role expectations	1 minute	
Contract ground rules	15 seconds	
Discuss agenda	30 seconds	
Body of the Meeting		
Review the four solutions decided on in previous meeting	15 minutes	
Develop an action-plan time line; E phase		
a. Identify the actions needed to implement the four solutions	25 minutes	
Break	**10 minutes**	
b. Clarify actions for understanding	15 minutes	
c. Eliminate actions that won't work	5 minutes	
d. Place the actions in sequential order	15 minutes	
e. Assign who is responsible for which action	15 minutes	
f. Assign a completion date for each action	10 minutes	
g. Reach a consensus on the actions	5 minutes	
End of the Meeting		
Summarize against the outcome	15 seconds	
Verify action items, set next meeting date	30 seconds	
Praise the group's effort	15 seconds	

When the meeting is over, the group can begin implementing its plan, which is shown in Figure A-7. This is the action-plan time line it will be following to reduce unnecessary truck rolls.

Now that the action-plan time line has been created and the group has made commitments to the action items and the time frames, Natalie's job for this portion of the effort has been accomplished. The group will need to continue to monitor its efforts to ensure that the members are meeting the objective that was set in the goal statement. Natalie will continue to monitor progress and be available to assist if needed.

Figure A-7. Action-Plan Time Line

Activity	1	2	3	4	5	Who
1. Get ideas for wording message to send to customers the night before service is scheduled	■					Ron Jay Frank
2. Create the message to be sent to customers	■					Ron, Jay Frank
3. Schedule vendor to set up the new message in the system		■				Ron
4. Have dispatch employees begin verifying customer directions and ordered services on all calls to customers as the truck is on the way	■					Tom
5. Meet with warehouse and tech departments to decide on the specific extra equipment each technician will need to provide additional service		■				Lana Bob Ann
6. Develop an inventory system to keep track of the extra equipment			■			Ann
7. Assign two technicians as floaters; create schedules, job responsibilities				■		Lana Larry
8. Inform CSRs and technicians of all the changes, along with other stakeholders			■			Ron Lana

Weeks

Summary

This section has given you a realistic example of how all the principles discussed in this book can come together to help you make improvements in your organization. Cable Express is a fictitious company, but this example shows many of the problems and challenges that real organizations face.

As you facilitate meetings in your own organization, remember the following points.

1. Use the PROBE model over the course of several meetings. It is very rare to get through all the phases of the model in only one meeting. Research and data collection typically must be done over a period of time between meetings.

2. The best route to the group's objective is always the simplest, most direct route. Use a minimum number of process tools to reach the intended outcome for each meeting.

3. Continue to remind the group of the overall goal statement, so they always keep the "big picture" in mind. For example, Cable Express was motivated to make changes because competitors were stealing customers away. The group can't afford to lose sight of the problem: if the improvements do not reduce significantly the time that customers wait for service, the group has more work yet to do.

Several very important principles are exemplified by the change effort at Cable Express. First, the responsibility for taking action does not rest only with the facilitator. Your group is responsible for its own success. As a facilitator, you can exert an influence, but the success the group experiences depends on the commitment and ability of its members. That's because organizations are successful because everyone takes part and contributes, from the top on down. No one person can carry the weight of an entire organization. It takes each individual working in concert with the others and putting forth his or her best effort. Virtually every person wants to be successful, but they don't always know how to be. As a facilitator, you can help by influencing meeting participants and making significant contributions to your organization. This case has illustrated one way to make this happen.

Appendix B

Tools and Templates

Meeting Planner

Objectives

▶ What do you want to achieve?

Background Information

▶ What do you already know?

▶ What do you need to know?

▶ What limits the group's ability to deal with deadlines, constraints, and available resources?

Meeting Participants

▶ Who would expect to be involved?

▶ Who needs information?

▶ Who can contribute or gain something from attending?

▶ Who has the authority to decide or the commitment needed?

▶ Who might resist?

Agenda Planning

▶ What topics do you want to cover?

▶ What do others want to cover?

▶ How long should the meeting last?

▶ Where is the meeting? When?

Best Medium

▶ Is the issue so sensitive that an in-person meeting is required?

▶ Will it be so difficult to get all participants together that a conference call is preferred?

▶ Will the expenses of an in-person meeting outweigh the importance of one?

Participant Preparation

▶ What information should you give ahead of time?

▶ How should people prepare before they come to the meeting?

Facility Arrangements

▶ What equipment is needed?

▶ How should the room be arranged? (classroom style, conference style, U-shape, tables)

▶ For conference calls, did you reserve the conference bridge and check the speakerphone?

Roles and Responsibilities

▶ Who is facilitating the meeting?

▶ Who is taking notes or tracking action items?

▶ Who is keeping track of time?

Meeting Outcome and Agenda Form
(for the person conducting the meeting)

Expected Outcome:

Date: _____
Time: _____
Place: _____
Who Should Attend:

What	Time	Guest Speakers
Beginning of the Meeting Welcome the group Clarify the outcome and overall goal Set role expectations Contract ground rules Discuss agenda	15 seconds 10 minutes 1 minute 15 seconds 30 seconds	
Body of the Meeting		
End of the Meeting		

Meeting Announcement

Please plan to attend the following meeting:
Date:
Time:
Location:
Purpose:
Bridge (for conference calls):

Tentative Agenda

Topic	Time	Guest Speaker

List of Participants:	What to Bring/Prepare for:

Questions/Issues to Consider:

Reaction/Response Chart

Possible Group Reaction	Your Response

Meeting Preparation To-Do List

Date Completed	Action Needed
	1. Write a specific and concise meeting outcome.
	2. Determine whether you will be sharing information or getting group input and decisions.
	3. Decide who needs to attend.
	4. Create the agenda.
	5. Decide what roles will be needed.
	6. Schedule the time and place and arrange for equipment and refreshments.
	7. Send out an announcement to leaders, stakeholders, and meeting participants to publicize the meeting. (Include the meeting outcome and agenda, ground rules, and any other visuals and the bridge number for conference calls.)
	8. Plan for possible reactions/responses from meeting participants.
	9. Create visuals, including the meeting announcement and ground rules on a flip chart.

Meeting Preparation To-Do List

Action to Be Taken	Who's Responsible	By When

Appendix C

Bibliography

Auvine, Brian, Betsy Densmore, Mary Extrom, Scott Poole, and Michel Shanklin. *A Manual for Group Facilitators*. Madison: Wisconsin Clearinghouse, 1978.

Conway, William E. *The Quality Secret: The Right Way to Manage*. Nashua, NH: Conway Quality, 1992.

Doyle, Michael, and David Straus. *How to Make Meetings Work*. New York: Jove Books, 1982.

Drew, Jeannine, *Mastering Meetings: Discovering the Hidden Potential of Effective Business Meetings*. 2nd edition. New York: McGraw-Hill, 1994.

Goldratt, Eliyahu M., and Jeff Cox. *The Goal: A Process of Ongoing Improvement*. Great Barrington, MA: North River Press, 1992.

Katzenbach, Jon R., and Douglas K. Smith. *The Wisdom of Teams: Creating the High-Performance Organization*. New York: HarperBusiness, 1994.

Kennedy, Robert F. *Thirteen Days, A Memoir of the Cuban Missile Crisis*. New York: Penguin Books USA, 1969.

Kinlaw, Dennis C. *Team-Managed Facilitation: Critical Skills for Developing Self-Sufficient Teams*. San Diego: Pfeiffer & Company, 1993.

Kiser, A. Glenn. *Masterful Facilitation: Becoming a Catalyst for Meaningful Change*. New York: AMACOM, 1998.

Leatherman, Dick. *The Training Trilogy—Facilitation Skills*. Amherst, MA: Human Resource Development Press, 1990.

Mosvick, Roger K., and Robert B. Nelson. *We've Got to Start Meeting Like This! A Guide to Successful Meeting Management*. Revised edition. Indianapolis: Park Avenue Productions, 1996.

Vaughan, Diane. *The Challenger Launch Decision: Risky Technology, Culture, and Deviance at NASA*. Chicago: University of Chicago Press, 1996.

Index